THE FALL AND RISE OF CHINA

The Fall and Rise of China
Healing the Trauma of History

PAUL U. UNSCHULD

REAKTION BOOKS

Published by Reaktion Books Ltd
33 Great Sutton Street
London EC1V 0DX, UK
www.reaktionbooks.co.uk

First published 2013

Translated by Nicolas Kumanoff

Printed and bound in Great Britain
by Bell & Bain, Glasgow

A catalogue record for this book
is available from the British Library

ISBN 978 1 78023 168 6

Contents

Introduction

A nation's past is easily forgotten –
and also not so easily forgotten
                    A Cheng 阿城

IN JANUARY 2011, when Hu Jintao, the president of the People's Republic of China, was welcomed by U.S. president Barack Obama on a state visit to Washington, DC, the official protocol conveyed the impression that here, two heads of state were meeting as equals. Pundits even called the Chinese leader 'the most powerful person in the world' – a designation long reserved for the American president.

During the preceding century and a half China had been consistently humiliated, first by the Western imperial powers and then even more by its smaller island neighbour, Japan. For a time the 'Middle Kingdom' seemed on the verge of becoming a pawn of foreign interests. Toward the close of the last imperial dynasty, internal conflicts further eroded the great country's global standing to its nadir.

Then, in a process probably unmatched in history, this great culture laid low by another, younger civilization recovered vigorously from its seemingly hopeless plight – so much so that today the state and its leaders, with its burgeoning economic and military might, are again globally acknowledged and not infrequently feared.

This Herculean task could only be accomplished because China, confronted by the evident superiority of Western science and technology, had committed to an unsparing self-diagnosis which identified the aspects of Western civilization the country had to adopt in order to remove the cultural impediments to China's own renaissance. Instead of venting its many individual aversions to the West as collective hatred of the aggressors, China took a path of reason and fundamental renewal.

In the course of their confrontation with Western culture, Chinese intellectuals and policy-makers swiftly recognized that their country could not hope to stand up to the imperialist powers simply by buying Western weapons and technology. Beginning in the early twentieth century, therefore, attention was lavished on the full spectrum of Western thinking. Discussions over how best to pull the country out of its misery quoted the most diverse philosophers from the past and present of both Europe and America. In the middle of the century, ongoing intellectual disputes and violent conflicts culminated in the People's Republic of China, which, gripped for two more decades by extremist political turmoil, itself appeared closer to economic oblivion than to a new age of regional – let alone global – dominance. Only from the early 1970s did China begin to reap the rewards of having examined its own cultural past and the Western civilization that was believed to be superior in so many ways.

The first half of this book traces the course of China's agony in the nineteenth and early twentieth centuries. The facts are familiar to anyone who knows the country; I have sequenced them here in a concise form.[1] The second half of the book explores a distinctive feature of China's resurgence that has not previously been identified as such. China sought responsibility for its predicament, as well as the healing of its collective trauma, exclusively within itself. The long-prevalent mentality in Europe of blaming one's own misfortune on the actual or alleged parties that caused it, and of demanding their future support, was and remains alien to China, irrespective of the country's adoption of Marxist thought and the Communist Party's leading role in society.

Profoundly wounded by both the Western nations and Japan, China prescribed for itself a therapy that followed the same principle that Chinese medicine uses in treating individual illnesses: the cause lies first and foremost within oneself. Evil can penetrate from outside only if one opens up a breach for it. Prevention and therapy must therefore always begin with one's own deficiencies and mistakes.

One can certainly characterize the patterns of China's relations with the West as a 'clash of cultures', but this struggle is not marked by terrorist attacks and counterstrikes. It is a quiet and subtle conflict, and it is still far from clear which side will be victorious.

PART I

China – Zhongguo – An Empire at the Centre of the World

ONE

A Distant King is Turned Away

AT THE INSTIGATION of the British East India Company, in 1793 George III sent a delegation to China led by Lord Macartney. The British hoped to persuade the Imperial Court in Beijing to open up the vast Chinese Empire to trade with Great Britain. Laden with gifts, Macartney presented an array of goods as evidence of the economic prowess that the British hoped would impress the emperor. For its part, the Chinese court sent ships and vehicles festooned with banners reading 'Embassy from the land of England for the delivery of tributes' for all to see, and received the English ambassadors with ritual ceremonies of epic dimensions. The emperor spoke personally with the English ambassador. In September, however, in two edicts, the monarch conveyed to Macartney his rejection of the British proposals.

The language used in these documents eloquently illustrates the air of impregnability surrounding the Emperor Qianlong (1711–1799), one of China's most glorious rulers, and how culturally superior the Chinese side felt. The lofty condescension with which Qianlong responded to the British petitions demonstrates the pride with which the alien Manchurian dynasty ruled its domains. After conquering China more than a century earlier the Manchu immediately recognized the greatness of the country's culture and civilization. Knowing that they were horsemen from the north who ruled over a glorious and ancient civilization in no way stopped them from broadly identifying with their dominions.

History is littered with episodes of invaders irretrievably destroying great and venerable cultures. The Manchu did not take that path. They knew the value of the treasure they had won control of, and in the succession of the emperors Kangxi (r. 1661–1722), Yongzheng (r. 1722–35) and Qianlong (r. 1735–

96, de facto until 1799) they led China to another golden age. Frontiers with neighbouring peoples were largely secured and relations with the Russian Tsarist regime handled to the benefit of both sides.

As the supreme ruler of the Middle Kingdom or *zhongguo*, Qianlong worded his reply to the British monarch with cool condescension, flatly rejecting Britain's request to extend trade beyond the small southern port of Macao and the city of Canton. For reasons that to this day remain less than comprehensible, China had abruptly ended a thoroughly promising foray into long-distance seafaring many years earlier and was utterly uninterested in other countries' products. In the eyes of the Manchu these were simple, superfluous trinkets of no benefit to China.

The edicts of Qianlong to George III speak for themselves. Given here complete, they began a process in which China first fell from the heights of cultural and economic greatness to the depths of subservience to foreign interests and finally – and uniquely among civilizations in decline – used its own strengths to rise back to power.

You, O King, live beyond the confines of many seas, nevertheless, impelled by your humble desire to partake of the benefits of our civilisation, you have dispatched a mission respectfully bearing your memorial. Your Envoy has crossed the seas and paid his respects at my Court on the anniversary of my birthday. To show your devotion, you have also sent offerings of your country's produce.

I have perused your memorial: the earnest terms in which it is couched reveal a respectful humility on your part, which is highly praiseworthy. In consideration of the fact that your Ambassador and his deputy have come a long way with your memorial and tribute, I have shown them high favour and have allowed them to be introduced into my presence. To manifest my indulgence, I have entertained them at a banquet and made them numerous gifts. I have also caused presents to be forwarded to the Naval Commander and six hundred of his officers and men, although they did not come to Peking, so that they too may share in my all-embracing kindness.

As to your entreaty to send one of your nationals to be accredited to my Celestial Court and to be in control of your country's trade with China, this request is contrary to all usage of my dynasty and cannot possibly be entertained. It is true that Europeans, in the service of the dynasty, have been permitted to live at Peking, but they are compelled to adopt Chinese dress, they are strictly confined to their own precincts and are never permitted to return home. You are presumably familiar with our dynastic regulations. Your proposed Envoy to my Court could not be placed in a position similar to that of European officials in Peking who are forbidden to leave China, nor could he, on the other hand, be allowed liberty of movement and the privilege of corresponding with his own country; so that you would gain nothing by his residence in our midst.

Moreover, our Celestial dynasty possesses vast territories, and tribute missions from the dependencies are provided for by the Department for Tributary States, which ministers to their wants and exercises strict control over their movements. It would be quite impossible to leave them to their own devices. Supposing that your Envoy should come to our Court, his language and national dress differ from that of our people, and there would be no place in which to bestow him. It may be suggested that he might imitate the Europeans permanently resident in Peking and adopt the dress and customs of China, but, it has never been our dynasty's wish to force people to do things unseemly and inconvenient. Besides, supposing I sent an Ambassador to reside in your country, how could you possibly make for him the requisite arrangements? Europe consists of many other nations besides your own: if each and all demanded to be represented at our Court, how could we possibly consent? The thing is utterly impracticable. How can our dynasty alter its whole procedure and system of etiquette, established for more than a century, in order to meet your individual views? If it be said that your object is to exercise control over your country's trade, your nationals have had full liberty to trade at Canton for many a year, and have received the greatest consideration at our hands. Missions have been sent by Portugal and Italy, preferring similar requests. The Throne appreciated their sincerity and loaded them with favours, besides authorising measures to facilitate their trade with China. You are no doubt aware that, when my Canton merchant, Wu Chao-ping, was in debt to the foreign ships, I made the Viceroy advance the monies due, out of the provincial treasury, and ordered him to punish the culprit severely. Why then should foreign nations advance this utterly unreasonable request to be represented at my Court? Peking is nearly two thousand miles from Canton, and at such a distance what possible control could any British representative exercise?

If you assert that your reverence for Our Celestial dynasty fills you with a desire to acquire our civilisation, our ceremonies and code of laws differ so completely from your own that, even if your Envoy were able to acquire the rudiments of our civilisation, you could not possibly transplant our manners and customs to your alien soil. Therefore, however adept the Envoy might become, nothing would be gained thereby.

Swaying the wide world, I have but one aim in view, namely, to maintain a perfect governance and to fulfil the duties of the State: strange and costly objects do not interest me. If I have commanded that the tribute offerings sent by you, O King, are to be accepted, this was solely in consideration for the spirit which prompted you to dispatch them from afar. Our dynasty's majestic virtue has penetrated unto every country under Heaven, and Kings of all nations have offered their costly tribute by land and sea. As your Ambassador can see for himself, we possess all things. I set no value on objects strange or ingenious, and have no use for your country's manufactures. This then is my answer to your request to appoint a representative at my Court, a request contrary to our dynastic usage, which would only result in inconvenience to yourself. I have expounded my wishes in detail and have commanded your tribute Envoys to leave in peace on their homeward journey. It behoves you, O King, to respect my sentiments and to display even greater devotion and loyalty in future, so that, by perpetual submission to our Throne, you may secure peace and prosperity for your country hereafter. Besides making gifts (of which I enclose an inventory) to each member of your Mission, I confer upon you, O King, valuable presents in excess of the number usually bestowed on such occasions, including silks and curios – a list of which is likewise enclosed. Do you reverently receive them and take note of my tender goodwill towards you! A special mandate.

You, O King, from afar have yearned after the blessings of our civilisation, and in your eagerness to come into touch with our converting influence have sent an Embassy across the sea bearing a memorial. I have already taken note of your respectful spirit of submission, have treated your mission with extreme favour and loaded it with gifts, besides issuing a mandate to you, O King, and honouring you with the bestowal of valuable presents. Thus has my indulgence been manifested.

Yesterday your Ambassador petitioned my Ministers to memorialise me regarding your trade with China, but his proposal is not consistent with our dynastic usage and cannot be entertained. Hitherto, all European nations, including your own country's barbarian merchants, have carried on their trade with our Celestial Empire at Canton. Such has been the procedure for many years, although our Celestial Empire possesses all things in prolific abundance and lacks no product within its own borders. There was therefore no need to import the manufactures of outside barbarians in exchange for our own produce. But as the tea, silk and porcelain which the Celestial Empire produces, are absolute necessities to European nations and to yourselves, we have permitted, as a signal mark of favour, that foreign hongs [merchant firms] should be established at Canton, so that your wants might be supplied and your country thus participate in our beneficence. But your Ambassador has now put forward new requests which completely fail to recognise the Throne's principle to 'treat strangers from afar with indulgence', and to exercise a pacifying control over barbarian tribes, the world over. Moreover, our dynasty, swaying the myriad races of the globe, extends the same benevolence towards all. Your England is not the only nation trading at Canton. If other nations, following your bad example, wrongfully importune my ear with further impossible requests, how will it be possible for me to treat them with easy indulgence? Nevertheless, I do not forget the lonely remoteness of your island, cut off from the world by intervening wastes of sea, nor do I overlook your excusable ignorance of the usages of our Celestial Empire. I have consequently commanded my Ministers to enlighten your Ambassador on the subject, and have ordered the departure of the mission. But I have doubts that, after your Envoy's return he may fail to acquaint you with my view in detail or that he may be lacking in lucidity, so that I shall now proceed . . . to issue my mandate on each question separately. In this way you will, I trust, comprehend my meaning . . .

Your request for a small island near Chusan, where your merchants may reside and goods be warehoused, arises from your desire to develop trade. As there are neither foreign hongs nor interpreters in or near Chusan, where none of your ships have ever called, such an island would be utterly useless for your purposes. Every inch of the territory of our Empire is marked on the map and the strictest vigilance is exercised over it all: even tiny islets and farlying sandbanks are clearly defined as part of the provinces to which they belong. Consider, moreover, that England is not the only barbarian land which wishes to establish . . . trade with our Empire: supposing that other nations were all to imitate your evil example and beseech me to present them each and all with a site for trading purposes, how could I possibly comply? This also is a flagrant infringement of the usage of my Empire and cannot possibly be entertained.

The next request, for a small site in the vicinity of Canton city, where your barbarian merchants may lodge or, alternatively, that there be no longer any restrictions over their movements at Aomen, has arisen from the following causes. Hitherto, the barbarian merchants of Europe have had a definite locality assigned to them at Aomen for residence and trade, and have been forbidden to encroach an inch beyond the limits assigned to that locality . . . . If these restrictions were withdrawn, friction would inevitably occur between the Chinese and your barbarian subjects, and the results would militate against the benevolent regard that I feel towards you. From every point of view, therefore, it is best that the regulations now in force should continue unchanged . . .

Regarding your nation's worship of the Lord of Heaven, it is the same religion as that of other European nations. Ever since the beginning of history, sage Emperors and wise rulers have bestowed on China a moral system and inculcated a code, which from time immemorial has been religiously observed by the myriads of my subjects. There has been no hankering after heterodox doctrines. Even the European (missionary) officials in my capital are forbidden to hold intercourse with Chinese subjects; they are restricted within the limits of their appointed residences, and may not go about propagating their religion. The distinction between Chinese and barbarian is most strict, and your Ambassador's request that barbarians shall be given full liberty to disseminate their religion is utterly unreasonable.

It may be, O King, that the above proposals have been wantonly made by your Ambassador on his own responsibility, or peradventure you yourself are ignorant of our dynastic regulations and had no intention of transgressing them when you expressed these wild ideas and hopes . . . . If, after the receipt of this explicit decree, you lightly give ear to the representations of your subordinates and allow your barbarian merchants to proceed to Chêkiang and Tientsin, with the object of landing and trading there, the ordinances of my Celestial Empire are strict in the extreme, and the local officials, both civil and military, are bound reverently to obey the law of the land. Should your vessels touch the shore, your merchants will assuredly never be permitted to land or to reside there, but will be subject to instant expulsion. In that event your barbarian merchants will have had a long journey for nothing. Do not say that you were not warned in due time! Tremblingly obey and show no negligence! A special mandate![2]

Twenty years later, in 1816, the British crown launched a second attempt to establish formal commercial relations with the Empire of China, to place the existing – and for the British, totally inadequate – exchange of goods on a broader footing. Lord Amherst, who would go on to become Governor-General of India, was sent to follow in the footsteps of the hapless Macartney. He did not get far. After landing in Baihe he negotiated with Chinese protocol officers over the terms of an audience with Emperor Jiaqing. Amherst refused to kowtow before the emperor – that act so despised among Europeans – unless the next Chinese official to visit the king in London agreed to likewise kneel and bow his head to the ground, so as to show the British crown the same level of regard. The Chinese declined and Amherst sailed away having accomplished nothing.

By then the British East India Company had for nearly a century been exclusively managing Britain's trade with China, which the Chinese strictly circumscribed. For various reasons, in 1834 the British government decided to revoke the private company's monopoly and place the China trade under state control. Lord Napier was appointed the first Superintendent of Trade in Canton and immediately set about provoking the Chinese.[3]

The British East India Company had always kept to the Chinese trade terms, which strictly forbade foreign traders from establishing direct contacts with the Chinese bureaucracy. Their designated counterparts and negotiating partners were an exclusive guild of Chinese merchants. This guild was in turn authorized to discuss any of the foreigners' concerns with the Chinese authorities. Ignoring these rules, Napier set out from Macao on 15 July 1834 for Canton to contact the Chinese viceroy there. At the gates of the city he conveyed to the local governor a letter that was rejected out of hand because it was not marked as a 'petition', as was demanded of emissaries from foreign states required to pay tributes. Napier refused to use this term, saying that it violated his country's honour. The Chinese official had little choice but to remain unyielding, otherwise he would probably have been put to death. When Napier stubbornly insisted on a direct meeting, the viceroy showed his annoyance. He fired Napier's Chinese servants, blocked all deliveries of food and drink and ordered soldiers to seal off the emissary's apartment.

Whereas the dismissal of Lord Macartney forty years earlier had been worded in condescending yet diplomatically polite language, the dispute between Governor Lu and Napier degenerated into an exchange of insults. In an announcement published in Canton, Lu first expressed outrage at the Englishman's gall for writing in terms that implied that the two sides were on equal terms. In a riposte likewise published in Canton, Napier accused the Chinese authorities of 'perverse' behaviour that would cause the 'ruin of thousands of hard-working Chinese who make their living by trading with Europeans.' Finally dropping all pretences of etiquette, Governor Lu again wrote publicly:

> A lawless foreign slave, Napier, has released a statement.[4] We have no idea how he, a barbaric dog of a foreign nation, could have the brazen insolence of presuming to call himself superintendent. As an alien, uncivilized superintendent and a person who finds himself in an official capacity, he should have at least the scantest understanding of decency and the law.[5]

On 2 September the governor ordered that all trade between the foreigners and the Chinese merchants in Canton be stopped. The costs for the British side now became too high and after three weeks, Napier left for Macao, empty-handed and red-faced. The Chinese were convinced that they had taught the British a lesson once and for all. The officials did not know that they had set off a chain of events that, far from just parrying insult, would become a turning point in Chinese history. Even during his standoff with Governor Lu, Napier vividly rendered the necessary consequences of the incident in his correspondence with Lord Palmerston at the Foreign Office:

> The governor has committed an outrage against the British Crown that will be paid back in kind . . . I can only beseech

Your Lordship once again to force [the Chinese side] to recognize my authority and the business of the king invested in me. If you can do this we will have no problem opening up the harbours.[6]

For a time, legal trade between Britain and China failed to advance after this incident. Meanwhile, an illegal process had been set in motion that could no longer be halted. Only a few more years would pass before the British lost their patience.

TWO

A Distant Pope is Expelled

THE BRITISH WERE neither the first nor the only European trading nation that tried to secure for themselves the promising markets and prized goods of East Asia. In 1516 the Portuguese landed in a small fishing village below the mouth of the Pearl River and, in 1557, established a permanent settlement that was tolerated because it acknowledged Chinese sovereignty. From 1680 a Portuguese governor headed the administration; the Chinese state received lease and tax revenues. In 1622 the Dutch attempted, unsuccessfully, to expel the Portuguese from Macao, as the settlement was called. In 1650 Dutch emissaries reached Beijing and had no complaints about being treated as representatives of a land required to pay tribute. Soon afterwards, the Dutch even helped the Empire to conquer the island of Formosa. From the viewpoint of the Chinese state, all these were simply marginal notes in their dealings with foreigners. During the reign of Emperor Kangxi (1661–1722), China's power and territorial extent were both near their historical zenith. His successor, the Emperor Qianlong, whose reign lasted more than six decades from 1735 to 1796, looked upon an empire whose greatness – in many respects – was unmatched by any other state in the world at the time.

In Europe the Industrial Revolution produced several more or less equally powerful nation states that could significantly increase their territory and population only in distant lands. On the East Asian mainland, no comparable balance of power developed. The colonies were right next door.

Over the course of two millennia the Han nation continually extended its power from its homeland along the Yellow River over a great number of other peoples, most of whom still live today as 'ethnic minorities', often in autonomous regions of

China. Some were forcibly subjugated by military means, others submitted to Han rule without resisting, and added to the size of the expanding Chinese empire. Not even the fact that China itself was defeated several times by neighbouring peoples during the second millennium could change this. Early in the twelfth century the Jurchen people overran northern China and in 1125 founded their own dynasty, which would last until the year 1224, when it was destroyed by another northern people, the Mongols. They went on to conquer China's south, extinguish the Song Dynasty and establish themselves in 1271 as the Yuan Dynasty. Only in 1368 did a Chinese revolt succeed in casting off the foreign hegemony and establish a new Chinese regime. The Ming Dynasty survived nearly three centuries until, in 1644, another nation of horsemen, the Manchu, again founded an alien regime. This would be the final dynasty of the 2,000-year imperial period, which was finally replaced by a republic in 1911. An enduring characteristic of all phases of foreign hegemony was the continued existence of Chinese civilization. All the alien nations that took power in China introduced only fragments of their own cultures into the great empire while subordinating themselves to its own cultural achievements. This was how the historically unparalleled continuity of the 'Chinese' Empire worked and survived, regardless of foreign rule.

Ultimately, at its territorial zenith under the Qing Dynasty of the Manchu, China had expanded beyond its regional core to include the homeland of the Manchu foreign hegemons, as well as Mongolia in the north, Turkic peoples in the west and Tibetans in the southwest. Moreover it collected tribute payments from Nepal, Burma, Laos, Siam, Annam, the Ryukyu Islands and Korea.

Russia was the first European state to conclude a treaty with China regulating commerce and border issues. Russian fur traders had penetrated ever further east and, to the consternation of the Chinese, set up small, fortified settlements in the border region near the Amur River. For a while the situation did not go beyond intermittent clashes with Chinese forces, as wars in the south placed greater demands on the attention of Chinese

generals. Only in 1685, when Cossacks began demanding tributes from Tungusic peoples in the form of fur animals, did the
Chinese overrun the oldest settlement, called Albasin by the
Europeans, destroy the fortifications and finally, in 1689, sign
the Treaty of Nerchinsk, which set the border, returned some
areas to China and regulated jurisdiction over people who had
committed crimes across the border. Following China's old
understanding of the balance of power, Russia was described in
the Chinese version of the treaty as a country required to pay
tribute. Following European custom, the Russian version treated
the two states as equals.

Two Jesuit priests, Jean-François Gerbillon and Thomas
Pereira, helped the Chinese negotiate with the Russians. Texts
were translated from Chinese into Latin and then into Russian
and vice versa. The Jesuits had come to East Asia as the first European religious community with the intention of converting the
Chinese infidels. Their erudition helped build many bridges
between Eastern and European science and civilization.

Near the end of the sixteenth century, Matteo Ricci became
the first Jesuit missionary to reach China. He and many later
members of the Society of Jesus impressed Chinese scholars and
even the emperor with their knowledge of mathematics, astronomy and geography. In return the missionaries likewise
honoured China's flourishing culture. In this way they managed
to secure the permission of their Jesuit superiors in Europe to
preach Christ's message in China in a manner marked by
accommodation, not confrontation. That meant, for example,
presenting the entire liturgy to the Chinese in their own
language instead of Latin, and respecting Chinese custom in
clothing. This approach helped them make the desired progress.

Scholars such as Adam Schall von Bell and Ferdinand
Verbiest enjoyed the highest esteem. The emperor himself took
lessons from these Europeans in subjects including astronomy,
and commissioned them to map out the empire. When the
Chinese fought a war against the Oirats over control of Mongolia from 1690 to 1696, the Jesuits also aided their hosts with
their knowledge of modern European military technology. The

Oirats had no weapons to respond to the Chinese cannons and muskets, and battles were decided quickly. The missionaries' many useful services and the monarch's receptive attitude culminated in 1692 in an edict of tolerance by the emperor. Construction of churches was permitted in certain areas and freedom of religion respected. By 1700 the missionaries could look upon a flock of at least 200,000 converted Chinese Christians.

At first glance the Jesuit mission appeared to be thoroughly successful, but an underlying conflict was brewing among the various Catholic orders active in China. The real motives behind the dispute, which would last more than a century and end in calamity, seem to have been the lesser orders' envy and resentment of the glory in which the Jesuits basked. The Portuguese reserved the right to manage the Church's activities in the Far East. In Europe, meanwhile, the Jesuits found themselves facing mounting suspicion that would climax in a complete ban. Yet the real cause was a philological problem.

How was one supposed to express 'God' in a language that had no corresponding concept and therefore no appropriate term? One obvious option was to choose the Chinese word *tian* and reinterpret it in the Christian sense. Literally translated, *tian* means 'sky' or 'heaven', but this heaven had long been ascribed powers to influence and change human lives on earth, similar to the powers the Christian faith ascribes to God. On Buddhist temples one occasionally encounters the inscription *ren suan bu ru tian suan*, which means 'heavenly plans stand above human plans.' Since ancient times, Chinese champions of existential autonomy countered this proverb with their own, such as *wo ming zai wo bu zai tian*, 'my fate lies in my hand, not in that of heaven.' Replacing 'heaven' with 'God' gives a sense of why *tian* could be considered appropriate.

The dispute that began as early as the 1620s expanded over the following decades into what became known as the Rites Controversy, in which the Jesuits' entire accommodationist approach came under question. A fundamental and fatal problem proved to be the inclusion of Chinese ancestor worship, and especially that of Confucius, in the religious rites of Chinese converts. By then the Jesuits had come to know the culture and mentality of their host country and generally supported this accommodation. They knew it was the only way they could gain acceptance and inclusion in the people's daily lives, and especially those of the elites.

Their rivals took an uncompromising stance. The Emperor Kangxi was long dead and Qianlong ruled over China when, in 1742, Pope Benedict XIV officially condemned the Chinese rites. Even Emperor Yongzheng, who succeeded Kangxi in 1722 and reigned for only thirteen years until 1735, had lost patience with most missionaries. He considered the Jesuits useful and so permitted them to continue serving him. The others were expelled from the country. Christianity was classified as a hostile religion and banned; Chinese converts were persecuted.

Envoys of the Pope who sought to convince Yongzhang's successor Qianlong of the correctness of the Vatican's decision caused additional annoyance, because in the Chinese view no foreigner, not even the Pope, could claim the right to enforce decrees against the emperor's will, let alone in defiance of fundamental Chinese morality. As a young man, Emperor Kangxi had ended the mass persecution of Christians right at the start of his reign in 1664. Although the Rites Controversy weighed on his friendship with the Jesuit scholars, he did not resume the oppression. For his part, Qianlong gave the missionaries a choice: either adapt and therefore embrace basic Chinese rites – a step he also required of Christian converts – or leave China. Most Jesuits obeyed the edict from Rome and departed. Only a handful were allowed to stay. Missionary activity came to a standstill.

For Emperor Qianlong the situation was clear. His grandfather Kangxi had given the Christians the chance to integrate into Chinese culture. A distant leader in Rome then objected and claimed the right to establish the Christian religion as an alien body that could not be reconciled with Chinese culture. For the emperor, the idea of a second society within his empire whose dominant culture was not Chinese was unthinkable. Restrictions on cultural diversity were again tightened.

THREE

An Emperor's Legacy is Erased

OVER THE CENTURIES, Chinese monarchs certainly knew that beyond their own civilization's frontiers, a variety of other high cultures and ways of life existed. Yet the question that was seldom, if ever, asked was: should we care? To those at the centre, how important was the periphery?

During the age of the Tang, in the eighth and ninth centuries, China's then-capital Chang'an was probably the most vibrant city on the Eurasian continent. Syrian Nestorian Christians, followers of Manichaeism and Zoroastrianism in Persia, Indian Buddhists, Jews, Arab Muslims and many other foreigners lived and traded with their Chinese hosts, practiced their religions and left numerous marks on Chinese arts and sciences.

For several centuries China's manufactures, especially its prized silks and ceramics, left the country along the Silk Road. Only gradually did a coastal shipping trade develop that would expand the country's commerce beyond the Arab world to East Africa. Beginning in the twelfth century China made a bid to control this export route to its own advantage. The Chinese studied Arab navigation techniques, learned how to read the positions of the stars in order to make journeys away from coastlines, and finally discovered the 'needle that points south' or *zhinanzhen*, the compass.

Changes in dynasties in no way interrupted the country's maritime development, both commercial and military. In the thirteenth century, under the Song, China's seafarers numbered more than 50,000. The subsequent Mongolian dynasty known in Chinese as the Yuan, under Kublai Khan, a grandson of Genghis Khan, went a step further. The newfound ability to launch ships of up to 300 tons with a capacity of 600 passengers helped lure the emperor into launching two invasions of Japan, which had refused his demands to submit voluntarily to the Mongol empire.

On the first occasion, in 1274, a fleet with some 30,000 troops landed on the islands of Kyushu and Tsushima and initially inflicted heavy losses on the defenders. Then, one night, a severe storm came up while the invaders were on board their ships. Ten thousand drowned and the survivors withdrew. In 1281 the Mongol rulers mounted another invasion with an even bigger armada. Chroniclers claimed that it encompassed 4,500 ships and 150,000 soldiers.

The Japanese again had luck on their side, or, as they saw it, the 'divine wind' or *kamikaze*. After initial battles on Kyushu Island, for which the Japanese were this time well prepared, another typhoon rendered the massive Chinese ships unmanoeuverable, pushing them on land and into the hands of the Japanese defenders, who immediately cut down most of the invaders. Probably two-thirds of the invasion army, or 100,000 men, lost their lives. These were China's first and only attempts to invade and conquer another country by sea. One should keep in mind, however, that at the time China was only one part of a vast empire under non-Chinese hegemons, and that the attempt to include Japan in this empire was an act of Kublai Khan's Mongol imperialism rather than a Chinese initiative.[7]

The monarchs of the subsequent Ming Dynasty drew their own lessons from this military disaster, which had played no small role in hastening their forerunners' demise. From then on China would seek 'colonies' in its immediate geographical vicinity, not overseas.

This did not mean that overseas regions were ignored. China's hegemony still had to be displayed as far away as possible. The empire either supported or installed foreign governments that recognized and paid tribute to China. The Ming emperor Zhu Di (r. 1402–1424) launched the most active phase of this brand of Chinese maritime activity. While personally leading military operations on land, the monarch sent his commander Zheng He on naval expeditions. Born to a non-Chinese southwestern ethnicity, Zheng He came to China as a child prisoner, was castrated, and later won the emperor's trust as a loyal eunuch during the wars of succession early in Zhu Di's reign. The emperor eventually named him commander of a fleet that, in seven epic voyages, surpassed all else in the history of seafaring.

In the year 1405, probably the greatest armada a country had ever assembled set sail from the Chinese port of Liujia. Sixty 'treasure ships' or *baochuan* with enormous keels of up to 135 m and beams of 55 m each mounted 24 bronze cannon to provide firepower. To transport the crews totalling 28,000 men, including mounted units, and safeguard the giant ships' military and material logistics, a retinue of junks accompanied each treasure ship, so that a fleet of more than 300 vessels sailed under Zheng He's command. Men skilled in ironworking, astronomy and navigation stood ready to address the manifold needs of a maritime expedition. Doctors, pharmacists and cooks ensured physical well-being; Buddhist monks and Muslim teachers cared for spiritual needs while bearing witness to the fact that for extended periods of its history, China was a place where religious communities willing to integrate could easily coexist.

Never before or since has a state made a comparable effort to pursue a variety of goals with a single fleet. Besides hunting down pirates and smugglers at sea and demonstrating grandeur and power on land, the expeditions primarily explored and opened trade relations with the lands they visited. Interpreters and experts on diplomatic protocol were on hand to seal closer ties with governments considered obedient and agree on future tribute payments to China. Less compliant rulers found themselves facing the soldiers, who might sometimes help a more 'enlightened' regime take power.

Seven times, in 1405, 1407, 1409, 1413, 1416, 1421 and 1430, Zheng He led his fleet through the South China Sea around present-day Vietnam to Java, Sumatra, Ceylon and India, and past Ormus in present-day Iran to Aden, Mogadishu and finally the region on the East African coast around what is today Kenya. Goods were traded wherever possible. The fleet carried great supplies of porcelain and silks, silver, bronze and other metal wares, tea and candles – the things that the Chinese expected to be in demand abroad. Returning to China, the ships carried coveted luxury items like gems, pearls and ivory, spices such as cinnamon and pepper, rare timber including black bamboo, medicinal herbs and exotic animals like elephants, lions, parrots and giraffes.

One might think that the voyagers' reports and prospects of ever-expanding trade would have convinced the Chinese monarchs of the usefulness of such contact with alien peoples. Yet events took a different turn. Emperor Zhu Di's reign marked the high point of foreign commerce. His death brought with it a sudden end to all of China's overseas ambitions, which have only recently begun to return. His successor, Emperor Zhu Gaozhi, imposed a complete moratorium on the very day he took the throne. And although his reign would last only a few months before he died, he dealt China's maritime activities a severe setback that immediately impacted on the country's influence and reputation abroad.

Zhu Gaozhi banned the previously rather carefree logging of entire forests for the construction of new ships and outlawed the repair of existing vessels. Even the still-seaworthy fleet was banned from sailing. When demonstrations of Chinese power suddenly stopped, the effects were felt rapidly. As soon as the fleet with its terrifying war paint and troops ready to land stopped appearing along distant shores, many rulers there considered themselves relieved of the obligation to send their tributes to China. Given these substantial losses, Zhu Gaozhi's successor, Emperor Zhu Zhanji, decided to dispatch Zheng He one more time.

The expedition of the year 1433 took the fleet as far as the Red Sea. After its return, however, elements in the imperial court opposing these voyages, and especially the huge effort they required, gained influence. By the end of the century, con-servatives succeeded in having the construction of ships with more than two masts declared a capital offence punishable by death. To ensure once and for all that the wide ocean remained an impassable frontier, in 1525 the authorities ordered the destruction of all seaworthy vessels. All that remained of Zheng He's once awe-inspiring fleet with its majestic treasure ships were some memories committed to paper. Even Zheng He's logbooks were burned. China was again content with itself, alone. The stage was set for the rebuffing of the envoys of Pope Clement xiv and King George iii two centuries later.

PART II

A Civilization in Free Fall

FOUR

The Breach and the Thief

CHINESE MEDICAL THEORY traces illness back to natural pathogenic factors penetrating into the body. Of course, the human body is a closed system, which heat, moisture, cold and wind – to name only the four most important natural factors – cannot simply pierce unaided. Heat, moisture, cold and wind have to find a gap – *xu* – in the defences into which they can embed themselves. Only then are they able to penetrate the body, establish themselves there and trigger all kinds of pathological consequences.

Therefore – according to the theory – the individual cannot permit this gap to materialize. By behaving appropriately, he or she can stay healthy. Preventative conduct, then, is the best protection against outside intruders. According to a common Chinese adage, those who place their trust in medicines for healing are like homeowners who repair the breach in their house's walls only after the thieves have entered. Another analogy would be to start digging a well only after one feels thirsty or beginning to forge weapons when the war is already raging – in other words, much too late.

Though it may have been economical in terms of extending the empire's hegemonic claims on land, China's destruction of its maritime capabilities in the sixteenth century left a gap where, as historical chance would have it, the European prowlers immediately found purchase, thereby commencing the beginning of the end for the Chinese Empire. Wind, cold, heat and so on are all eminently useful as long as they contribute to the natural growth and decay of things outside the human organism. Once they find a hole and enter an alien organism where they do not belong, then the good becomes the bad, crippling the involuntary host.

It was the same process with the Europeans, who from the fifteenth century sailed to sea, scouting coastlines, learning to cross oceans, penetrating where they did not belong and establishing themselves on foreign soil to exploit their involuntary host countries. The Portuguese, Spanish, Dutch and British, the first maritime nations that struck out onto the high seas, were well-liked and civilized as long as they remained in their ancestral regions. As soon as they invaded other lands they morphed into personified evil, causing the most appalling and enduring traumas and destroying or at least profoundly harming indigenous life. When the Chinese, one of the more distant targets of this mischief, recognized this and searched for ways to heal their wounds, it was already almost too late. The moment they had declared the logbooks of Zheng He to be waste paper and committed them to the flames, they had opened the breach in their own house wall.

The European powers' depredations in North and South America, Africa, Southeast Asia and finally East Asia have been amply documented. Portugal and Spain led the way into the era of European colonialism. Unlike Russia and China, which could keep expanding into their immediate periphery without encountering nations able to stem their advance, European states had to cross the seas to subjugate other peoples and take possession of their natural and mineral resources. Even a country as diminutive as the Netherlands could capitalize on the administrative, economic and technological gulf between Europe and non-European regions to occupy territories many times larger than its own geographical size. France and Britain followed, finally becoming the mightiest colonial powers of all. The Germans, whose country was unified only in 1871, joined late. Yet they still had nearly five decades in which to add to the calamities that Europe's overseas expansion caused practically everywhere it went.

The causes of this process were varied. The quest for grandeur, keen competition – first among feudal states and later nation-states – as well as population pressures in some parts of Europe stimulated the exploitation (always enthusiastically supported by national clergies) of foreign resources. With its sense of the white man's superiority, the world-view these states espoused likewise justified violence. Once secured, the resources fuelled – first and foremost in the United Kingdom – the rise of great industries that in turn became the driving forces behind the opening of global markets. Demand for the riches of East Asia stimulated improvements in navigation. The old land routes had been blocked after the Ottoman conquest of Constantinople in the mid-fifteenth century. Trade monopolies belonging to a handful of Mediterranean city-states required that alternative routes take enormous detours around Africa's southern cape. The 'discovery' of North America itself came about through efforts to find an unimpeded route to East Asia. Technological advances from Arab and Persian cultures found their way to Europe, resulting in the evolution of Viking longships and Mediterranean galleys, suitable mainly for voyages close to coastlines, and the cogs with various mast sizes that greatly reduced the risks of oceangoing travel.

From its beginnings in 1513, the tiny Portuguese outpost of Macao was tolerated by Chinese authorities for more than three centuries. Only in 1849 did Portugal declare its colony independent of China. After some limited military engagements, it took until 1887 for the Chinese, weakened by domestic and external afflictions, to finally recognize Portuguese sovereignty over Macao.

The mainland Chinese paid little attention when in 1582 the Portuguese, in 1624 the Dutch and, two years later, the Spanish occupied Formosa, an island off the coast of the Chinese province of Fujian populated chiefly by peoples of Malay origin. These pinpricks off the empire's southeast coastline were still too small and insignificant. More of a nuisance was the retreat of some loyalists of the fallen Ming Dynasty to the island that the Chinese call Taiwan in the mid-seventeenth century. In 1683 forces of the Manchu Qing Dynasty invaded the island and drove out the Europeans.

For China, dealing with irksome barbarians from who knows where who cause trouble along this or that coastline through piracy or pillage was nothing new. The Europeans were regarded as exactly that kind of temporary coastal nuisance when they appeared off the empire's shores. Yet this time the Chinese were wrong. The British had bigger goals in mind, especially after taking control of India with relatively little difficulty. Their attention had turned to the even bigger prize of China.

Precious Chinese goods had been brought to Europe by land or sea ever since Roman times. With the dawn of the modern age, interest in China's manufactures rose again. Porcelain and silks were especially popular among European royal courts and those commoners able to afford them. Even imitations of Chinese porcelain and fine arts, furniture and handicrafts – high-quality fakes known as chinoiserie – flooded Europe. Chinese producers responded with porcelain designs adapted to what they supposed were European tastes and sold huge quantities of goods they called 'export porcelain' to European buyers in commercial ports, especially Manila. Since maritime navigation was officially banned for Chinese merchants, foreign ships (and smugglers) provided transportation. The Dutch East India Company and, later, the British East India Company dominated the business.

Besides the perennial bestsellers – tea, silk and porcelain – ceramics, spices, lacquers and fine cotton cloth also made their way from China to Europe to supply an ever-growing market. In 1761, for example, the British East India Company moved more than 2.5 million lb (11.3 million kg) of tea worth over £830,000 to Europe. In 1794 the British government drastically cut import taxes on tea, producing a corresponding jump in Chinese exports. In 1800 more than 3.5 million lb (15.9 million kg) of tea left the country for Europe.

On the other hand, no European product generated comparable interest, and therefore demand, in China. The country imported tin, copper, lead and woollens, but these products did not even begin to offset the Europeans' trade deficit with China. In the early nineteenth century some 200 European merchant ships landed annually in the commercial centre of Canton. On the voyage to China they carried 90 per cent ballast in their holds. Silver was the only equivalent value that could offset that of the Chinese treasures. It has been estimated that between 1719 and 1833 Chinese merchants took in coins equalling 6,000 tons of pure silver for their exports.

This skewed trade was unfortunate in several respects. It forced the advent of the first global trading network that bound China with Europe, the u.s. and the Spanish colonies in Central and South America. The silver was mined in the Americas and then brought across the Pacific to Manila, where Chinese merchants accepted it as payment for their wares. These goods were then shipped to Europe, which was also conducting a growing trade with America. For many decades the system functioned fairly well, but the disadvantages of payment in silver grew increasingly onerous, as production and transport of the precious metal grew prohibitively expensive. Then a solution to the dilemma seemed to be found: opium.

The Portuguese were the first Europeans to import Indian opium, initially mixed with tobacco, to Taiwan, from where it continued on to the Chinese mainland. Chinese medicine took note of opium as early as the Tang era in the eighth century, in the recipe for the legendary antidote theriac, which was first manufactured under the ancient king Mithridates vi of Pontus (*c.* 132–63 BCE) and would go on to become one of the most widespread medicines in the European pharmacopoeia. Yet the composition of the medicine remained unknown to Chinese doctors. In the seventeenth and eighteenth centuries the rapid expansion of pure opium, whose early names *a-fu-rong* and *ya-pien* mimicked the drug's foreign name, likewise took place through pharmacy. The wealthier classes could afford opium as a sexual stimulant. Its use would not end there.

Over time, opium abuse spread through all social classes with devastating effects. The thieves found the breach and swarmed in. Chinese authorities became aware of the crisis only slowly. Another complicating factor was that in China, neither end users nor the countless individuals who profited from the various stages of the trade had any interest in stemming the drug's constantly expanding importation.

An imperial ban from 1729 calling opium a product that 'cunning barbarians sell to Chinese so as to swindle their money' had no notable effect. At that point 200 cases of opium, each weighing 63.5 kg, were entering the Chinese mainland annually. Sales and use in China climbed slowly at first. By 1773 imports had increased fivefold to (still only) 1,000 cases. With the forcible removal of the Dutch from India and Bengal and Britain's de facto attainment of a trade monopoly over Bengali opium, the foundation had been laid for expanded opium production and the use of this economical and easily transportable narcotic as an ideal currency for the China trade – ideal because it was the first, and so far, the only, product that seemed capable of gaining the entire Chinese population as users.

By 1790 the volume of opium exported annually to China from India had further quadrupled to 4,000 cases. The scruples of some British parliamentarians who banned the (still legal) importation of opium to China by the East India Company in 1784, forcing the company to hand the lucrative trade over to private merchants, proved only a temporary obstacle to the unrestricted expansion of opium as a means of payment in China. Profits from opium trafficking still flowed into the British East India Company's coffers, flimsily disguised as licensing fees paid by the private traders.

On the Chinese side the merchants authorized to deal with the Europeans were also quick to see the prospects offered by selling the contraband on the mainland. Many illicit networks were set up on both sides. Even American merchants got involved in the business, shipping opium from Persia and Turkey to China. Between 1775 and 1795 a full one-third of the British East India Company's total revenue came from licence fees paid by private opium merchants. By the time the Chinese emperor outlawed the use of opium in 1796 and its trade in 1800, the structures had become so well established, and the profits so lucrative for all concerned, that the imperial prohibitions were doomed to fail.

Moreover, to the delight of the British, the flow of silver in the China trade was changing direction. In 1807 the British East

India Company recorded the movement of 3.4 million silver pesos from Canton to Calcutta. Less than two decades later there was already a net outflow of silver from China. By this time the East India Company had lost its opium monopoly. Numerous European and American trading companies competed to sell opium in China. Once again, in 1813, the far-away imperial court tried to stop opium imports by tightening penalties – and failed again.

A few years later opium supplanted cotton as China's leading import. To escape state repression, in 1821 Chinese merchants founded a big depot at the mouth of the Pearl River, beyond the reach of the governor of Canton, who had been appointed to enforce the ban. In 1832 the quantity smuggled into the country climbed to 23,570 cases and in 1838 to more than 30,000.

The profits from the opium trade with China are well documented, especially those of Britain. Poppy cultivation and opium sales helped fill British coffers. The East India Company saw its revenues from the contraband trade grow exponentially, from 2.3 million rupees in 1800 and 8.2 million in 1815 to nearly 30 million by 1838. Given numbers like these, the House of Commons in London was utterly unwilling to bow to the critics of this 'immoral' trade and obstruct the cultivation of opium in the Southeast Asian colonies. Again and again, groups in the UK tried to put a stop to their country's involvement in opium smuggling. Yet the opium trade, which continued to expand unchecked for decades, illustrates clearly how dependent lawmakers had become on commercial macro-interests.

Profits from the drug trade helped Britain to finance the purchase of raw materials from the United States for its cotton industry around Manchester and the administration of its colony in India and the more recent colonies in Singapore and Hong Kong. The effects an abrupt end to these cash flows would have for the overall British economy so frightened policymakers in London that only in 1907, after substantial quantities of opium were being produced in China itself, would a Sino-British treaty be concluded that enshrined the complete end of British deliveries within the next ten years. The U.S. government, which drew far less advantage from the opium trade than the British, forced American merchants to get out of the opium business as early as 1880.

FIVE

The British Intervention: *Trauma 1*

AS TIME PASSED, the effects of opium smuggling and abuse became as destructive for China and its economy as they were lucrative for foreign countries and companies. The encounter with opium sent countless Chinese down a path lined with multiple dependencies. The far-away beneficiaries of opium smuggling tried to allay the European public's concerns by claiming that opium consumption in China could be compared with the enjoyment of alcoholic beverages in Britain or France. The reality was far different. Opium did far greater damage to the bodies and minds of addicts than alcohol did. The ranks of addicts swelled rapidly, with catastrophic effects on the state. Significantly, great numbers of soldiers as well as lower- and mid-level civil servants fell victim to the drug and were no longer capable of carrying out their duties.

The importing of opium also seriously threatened the structures of China's economy. The massive influx of silver, before opium was discovered as an ideal (from the British viewpoint) means of payment, had devalued copper coins as the standard unit of exchange, thereby driving up the cost of living for all those unable to get their hands on silver. After opium trafficking soon reversed the flow of silver out of the country, China's systems of payment and taxation began to fall apart. Revenue from agricultural goods fell steeply, causing huge numbers of farmers to lose their land after being unable to service their debts. As more and more land fell into the hands of a small number of magnates, independent peasants were reduced to being simple labourers or lost their livelihoods altogether. Poorer classes spent much of their money on opium, leaving little for other expenditure. Trade in these goods, and with it merchants' revenues, fell steeply. Therefore state tax revenue also dropped, while the tax burden on the individual – which still had to be paid in silver – grew.

Only at the beginning of the 1830s did the imperial central government recognize the threat to the state. The bureaucratic leaders in Beijing spent several years, from 1836 to 1839, discussing which steps would best put a stop to the scourge. Opium imports had to be suppressed and the silver outflow mitigated. Finally, in 1839, the administration in Beijing agreed on a programme of vigorous countermeasures. A dramatic struggle ensued between the Chinese Empire, which saw its existence threatened, and small, far-away Britain, fighting for its own economic interests. A chain of events also began that in the space of only seven decades would prostrate a civilization that for the previous two millennia had been at least the equal of any other political entity on the Eurasian continent.

Beijing appointed Lin Zexu (1785–1850) as the emperor's special commissioner to clean up Canton. Lin Zexu worked at the elite Hanlin Academy before climbing through various administrative positions which, given his moral integrity, took him as high as the office of governor-general of Hunan and Hubei provinces. He was fully aware of opium's destructive qualities and saw no other way of halting the scourge than by having opium growers and traffickers beheaded. The Confucians regarded this as the most demeaning kind of execution, as it involved the severing of a body part. The addicts were strangled – a more considerate means of killing, as the executed could still face his ancestors in the afterworld with an intact body.[8]

When Lin Zexu arrived in Canton on 10 March 1839 on the emperor's orders, he took steps directed at both the Chinese population and foreign profiteers. In a broad publicity campaign he warned Chinese users of the narcotic's dangers and ordered them to surrender their opium and paraphernalia, especially pipes, to the authorities within two months. He also called on the populace to report dealers and traffickers. He used the long-standing technique of dividing social cohorts especially prone to using opium – soldiers, exam candidates and others – into small groups of five people, each of whom were responsible for monitoring and, if necessary, reporting each other to the authorities. Within the next four months, more than 1,600 Chinese were arrested and 73,000 kilos of opium and 70,000 opium pipes had been confiscated.

Lin Zexu also took up his campaign with foreigners, at first using moral appeals. Among the British his counterpart as trade commissioner was Sir Charles Elliot (1801–1875), successor to the luckless Lord Napier, who had died shortly after returning from Macao. Elliot, who was born in Dresden, was active as a British naval officer in Europe, Africa and the Caribbean, where as 'Protector of Slaves' he was responsible for enforcing laws protecting the local bondsmen. In 1834 he was ordered to China as Napier's assistant, taking over his superior's position two years later. Lin Zexu appealed to Elliot and his merchants to stop importing opium, even writing a letter to Queen Victoria pointing out that, since opium was also banned in the UK, she should outlaw its exportation to China. The letter concluded: 'even though the barbarians may not necessarily intend to do us harm, yet in coveting profit to an extreme, they have no regard for injuring others. Let us ask, where is your conscience?'[9] A reply never came. The letter probably never even reached the queen.

Consequently, Lin Zexu took action. He gave the foreign merchants an ultimatum to hand over their opium stores to the Chinese authorities and immediately stop trading in the drug. When the foreigners refused, on 24 March 1834 he had them arrested in their factories – 350 men in all, including their high representative Elliot – and ordered Chinese merchants to terminate their contracts with them. The entire export trade in Canton came to a standstill. Elliot held out for six weeks. Then he consented to have the foreign traders' entire opium supplies handed over to the British Crown in return for debt certificates, and surrendered 1.4 million kg of opium to the Chinese. This way the subsequent actions of the Chinese would be directed not against private businessmen but the property of the British Crown, thereby justifying an official response to protect British interests, especially since Lin Zexu had not shied away from imprisoning a senior British official.

In a solemn ceremony on 3 June 1839, Lin Zexu asked the Spirit of the South Sea for forgiveness for an act that would greatly pollute its realm, and had 20,000 cases of confiscated opium dumped into the ocean. Once again the Chinese side had no idea that this would not be the end of the matter. Lin Zexu notified the emperor that the foreigners had been deeply ashamed and had stopped their misdeeds. He did not know he had given hardliners on the other side a welcome excuse to forcibly open the gates to China once and for all, and to reap the same riches there as were claimed for the British Empire elsewhere in the world. The outcome of the ensuing First Opium War, besides humiliating China, also spelled disaster for the once-esteemed Lin Zexu. He was stripped of all his offices and exiled to China's extreme northwest. Only after the death of Emperor Daoguang in 1845 could he return to Beijing and be rehabilitated.

The British Parliament initially refused to sanction military action against the Chinese Empire, but in 1840 a fleet was dispatched that arrived in China in June of that year. Some ships were left behind to blockade the port of Canton while the main body sailed farther north. The Chinese had no craft capable of engaging the modern British steamships. When the fleet arrived at Fort Dagu off the coast of Tianjin, the two sides met to negotiate. The British agreed to retreat to Canton.

Of course the agreement's terms satisfied neither the Chinese emperor nor the British Foreign Secretary, Lord Palmerston, who dismissed Elliot and replaced him with Sir Henry Pottinger as the Crown's plenipotentiary. Meanwhile the British fleet had become involved in minor engagements. The first British attacks on the coast took place under Pottinger's command. Pottinger captured Xiamen, Ningbo and Zhoushan. Reinforcements enabled the British to capture Shanghai and Zhenjiang. When the Chinese saw that the city of Nanjing was likewise about to fall to the British, they agreed to open peace talks. The resulting Treaty of Nanjing was signed in 1842, with a supplementary treaty a year later.

The conditions that the British demanded in return for halting military operations were strict. There was no longer any sign of the distant, insignificant king George III, whose envoys, having knocked in vain at the gates of paradise, were cordially but firmly sent packing. This time the victor dictated to the vanquished how relations would be conducted from then on, and the victor, to the dismay of the Chinese leadership, was none other than the faraway barbarian British king.

Would this just repeat a process that was anything but unusual in Chinese dynastic history? Would a regime (and a foreign one, the Manchu, at that) be replaced by a new dynasty that, awestruck by the country and above all its culture, would become more Chinese than the Chinese themselves, like Kangxi and Qianlong, and further add to the empire's glory? This time, the outcome was different. First, the invaders humiliated the Chinese by imposing the first of the so-called Unequal Treaties. Its central conditions were:

- The abolition of the system of Chinese merchant guilds as sole agents and intermediaries for foreign merchants
- Imposition of a 5 per cent import tariff
- Cession 'in perpetuity' of Hong Kong
- Compensation totalling $6 million in silver dollars for the opium destroyed by Lin Zexu
- $12 million in silver dollars in war indemnities
- Opening of five cities to free trade with foreign traders permitted to open representations there
- Permission to station British gunboats in the treaty ports
- Legal extraterritoriality for Britons
- Most favoured trading status: all privileges that China warded to other countries counted automatically for Britain as well

This treaty was the first to impose two systems of law and the authority of a foreign country on Chinese territory. The actual cause, the opium trade, was not mentioned in the text. Yet the abolition of the system of Chinese contract merchants further weakened the Chinese state's already feeble control over the drug's influx. Opium smuggling flourished.

The door to China had been opened. Not very wide, but well beyond what the Emperor Qianlong and his successors would ever have imagined. China was paying the price for its sixteenth century decision to abandon active seafaring, a decision that culminated in the burning of Zheng He's logbooks. China no longer had a high-seas naval capability nor the technological know-how to build one. Therefore it had no strategy for using a fleet. This was the breach into which the Europeans now rushed.

The British were the first to force the breach and immediately set about ruthlessly expanding their access. Other European states and the u.s. did not stand by idly for long. All of them now did what they could to secure a slice of the coveted cake.

With its own pact in 1844 the u.s. gained access to the same five treaty ports that the British had opened. The Americans also demanded and got extraterritoriality for their citizens, not only in criminal cases but in certain cases of civil law. That same year the French moved in, demanding the same rights as the Americans. Soon they managed to force an imperial edict permitting construction of Catholic churches in the treaty port cities. Chinese people were henceforth allowed to convert to Catholicism. In 1845 the edict's terms were expanded to include the Protestant faiths. One year later, in 1846, the edict was reaffirmed, with the French also securing the return of those Catholic churches that had been built under Emperor Kangxi and confiscated by the Chinese in the ensuing decades.

For China the war's outcome, with all the concessions to the European invaders it necessitated, was the first of many deep wounds that would eventually sever the continuity, unique in the world, of the political and cultural structures of the Chinese Empire that had survived for more than 2,000 years. The violation of its sovereignty and its manifest military inferiority drew more foreign intruders. In 1845 the Belgians gained trading rights; in 1847 the Swedes and Norwegians followed.

China's foreign Manchu rulers also found themselves under mounting domestic pressure. The fruitful domestic and foreign policies of the great Qing emperors Kangxi and Qianlong had become ancient lore. Multiple domestic problems were eroding the dynasty's legitimacy and ultimately prevented the empire from facing its external threats with national unity. The inner deterioration of the Manchu Dynasty's power contributed to the demise of China's imperial age. The fact was that Chinese civilization as such, in its civilian and military technology, its sciences and medicine, had failed to keep pace with progress in the u.s. and Europe.

For centuries, every Chinese dynasty lived with secret organizations in its realm whose founders preached revolutionary doctrines culled from various religions and attitudes. Such groups or movements found themselves in growing favour when dynasties were in decline, following natural disasters, farmers' migrations or the impoverishment of entire regions or populations. Sometimes even members of the bureaucracy or the intelligentsia found reasons for joining or supporting a secret society.

A syncretistic doctrine, combining elements of Buddhism, Daoism and Manichaeism, arose in the early twelfth century in Suzhou. It appealed to disenfranchised farmers, small merchants and other distressed economic groups. Members pledged to keep a vegetarian diet. They refused to give the state tax money or serve in its armed forces. Its founder, Mao Ziyuan, taught that many signs, especially disasters, announced the approaching return of the Buddha Maitreya. The new doctrine became known as the 'White Lotus'.

Several times in the following centuries new groups were founded that occasionally took up arms and tried to topple the prevailing order. One example was the rebellion of the Red Turbans in the early fourteenth century, which was aimed first against wealthy magnates and then took a nationalist turn against the alien Mongol rulers and, under the leadership of Zhu Yuanzhang, the son of impoverished peasants, overthrew the Yuan dynasty. Zhu Yuanzhang was proclaimed the first emperor of the (again Chinese) Ming Dynasty.

After close surveillance by the Ming rulers and the early Qing Dynasty had left the secret societies little space to grow and pushed them into a nearly invisible underground existence, their fortunes changed in the later eighteenth century. The usual maladies – mostly the rise of taxes and corruption – that generally accompany a long succession of rulers from the same family were combined with exceptionally rapid population growth and a lack of farmland. The devaluation of copper against the rising value of silver further complicated the payment of debts while demonstrating how the domestic crisis was linked to the European-driven opium trade. Countless Chinese attempted to escape the emergency and resettled in Southeast Asia, but for China a discharge valve on a par with Europe's – emigration to North America – did not exist.

The impoverishment of entire territories that always went hand-in-hand with profits for many large-scale property owners finally lit the fuse for which the secret societies had been waiting. From the late eighteenth to the early twentieth century, uprisings shook the empire and, together with the effects of the European invasions, left the Qing rulers helpless. The cultural structures of the Manchu Dynasty, which early on made the glory of Chinese civilization shine even more brightly, were too rigid, helpless and bereft of every kind of creativity to respond adequately to the challenges facing China from inside and out.

The so-called Wang Lun Uprising in 1774 lasted nearly three decades until Qing troops finally extinguished it in 1803. In 1811 another revolt drawing on the White Lotus ideology seemed close to succeeding. In 1813 the rebellion, now called the 'Teachings of the Heavenly Order', managed to penetrate the palace. Emperor Jiaqing was rescued at the last minute from death by his son, the subsequent emperor Daoguang. The biggest threat to the dynasty, however, would be the Taiping Rebellion, as it has come to be known.

SIX

The Taiping Rebellion

WITH AN ESTIMATED 20 to 30 million deaths, the Taiping Rebellion is considered the bloodiest civil war in recorded history. The revolt's base was the southern Chinese province of Guangxi, where several factors came together. They included discontented, non-Han-Chinese ethnicities that resented what they regarded as the aggressive expansion into their territories of Han Chinese, who strongly discriminated against indigenous peoples. In addition there was social and economic turbulence throughout southern China resulting from the rise of Shanghai, once an utterly insignificant harbour town, at the expense of Canton. The jobless could be won over for revolutionary causes just as easily as the soldiers idled after the Opium War and the inhabitants of riverfront regions were exposed to the depredations both of pirates and the ever-advancing Europeans. The bureaucracy of the faraway Manchu rulers was too corrupt and inefficient to enforce law and order. Underground groups, the best organized of which was the 'White Lotus', repeatedly capitalized on this explosive situation. For centuries they had been indoctrinated to take advantage of any conflict among the various ethnicities and any rebellious upheaval they believed suited their purposes. As was the case in previous uprisings, local conflicts and restive populations sparked the Taiping Rebellion. It needed a clever and charismatic leader to expand them into a national movement against the alien Manchurian elite.

Hong Xiuquan (1814–1864) was the man who personified the Taiping Rebellion. He failed several times to pass the exams that gave access to a career in the imperial administration. Given this and what else we know about him, it is tempting to attribute the physical illnesses and mental delusions of his later years to this inability to escape his hardscrabble existence as a teacher for a career of distinction. If we give credence to his reports, during one of his morbid episodes he saw a middle-aged man and a bearded old man on a throne. When a Christian missionary pamphlet later fell into his hands, he recognized the two: God the Son and God the Father. From that moment on he considered himself the younger brother of Jesus Christ.

Hong Xiuquan's education allowed him to construct another of the many syncretistic ideologies that Chinese heterodoxy has produced so plentifully until the present day. He blithely melded Christian doctrine with Confucian, Daoist and Buddhist ideas. This seemingly random conflation of religious and political revolutionary thought found its first enthusiastic reception among the Hakka, a widely scattered and therefore defenceless ethnic group that could not – unlike other threatened peoples – form its own militia. Only once the movement turned against the Qing rulers, whom it condemned as diabolical, alien and cruel, did it gain the mass support that would plunge the entire country into turmoil for years and nearly terminate the Manchu Dynasty in the mid-nineteenth century.

In 1853, in a series of merciless campaigns by gigantic armies over enormous distances, the 'Heavenly Kingdom of Great Peace' that Hong Xiuquan had proclaimed two years before took control of Nanjing. The imperial forces suffered one setback after another. When Shanghai appeared threatened in 1860, the British and French saw their own interests at risk. They had nothing to gain from a China ruled by the Taiping. They distrusted the movement's ideological cocktail of traditional Chinese ideas and Christian elements, and rejected as blasphemous Hong Xiuquan's portrayal of himself as Jesus' younger brother. Moreover the rebels' moral standards were unsuitable for winning allies among the troops in the treaty ports. The Taiping rejected private property. They gave the sexes equal rights while simultaneously demanding their strict separation. They condemned gambling, tobacco, alcohol, polygamy, slavery, prostitution and of course opium, which was why the Europeans had fought China in the first place.

The chaos that was evident throughout the administration of the 'Heavenly Kingdom of Great Peace' also left the Europeans in doubt that a Taiping victory would let them pursue their interests as efficiently as they could under the Qing. The officially neutral British and French therefore intervened in the defence of Shanghai, repulsing the advancing Taiping forces. Expecting little resistance, these had approached in relatively small numbers in any case. The Chinese elites also increasingly used European mercenaries for security.

Flawed strategy, egocentric power struggles among the Taiping commanders, and finally Hong Xiuquan's political agenda, which proved utterly inadequate to effectively govern the territories he conquered, were the reasons the enormous revolutionary potential that had put huge bodies of men in motion did not suffice to bring the Taiping victory. Once again the Qing bureaucracy, which repeatedly seemed finished during the uprising, managed to stabilize itself. In 1864, the imperial commander Zeng Guofan reported the situation was under control. Some regions remained restive; indeed, the dynasty would never again see a time of complete peace. Most of the blows that set the giant teetering anew were dealt from outside. They further weakened a structure that had already become hollowed out. When the first members of the elite recognized the danger, they declared that 'The Chinese building of ideas exists in its substance; the Western building of ideas exists in its use.' Yet the substance they were invoking had largely ceased to exist.

In retrospect, the Taiping Rebellion was shocking evidence of the multiple domestic woes besetting China. It also demonstrated that most of these, if not all, were caused or at least worsened by the conflict with the Europeans. In the course of the Taiping Rebellion revolutionary social, ethnic, military, religious and not least commercial interests soon gave rise to an insoluble jumble of alliances.

Adding to the blows from the Western imperialist powers that the Chinese Empire sustained in quick succession in the nineteenth and early twentieth centuries, the Taiping Rebellion was an internal wound that hastened the end of the Manchu Dynasty and thereby the Chinese imperial system as a whole.

SEVEN

The British-French Intervention:
Trauma 2

AS WE HAVE SEEN, the expansion of contraband opium imports to China progressed without the Chinese government managing to take effective countermeasures. Wherever the British considered such steps hostile to their own ends, they immediately responded with armed force.

On 8 October 1856 the British used the so-called Arrow Incident to bolster their position in China. The *Arrow* was a Chinese ship registered in Hong Kong and flying the British flag. Chinese authorities had reason to suspect that the ship was smuggling opium into China. When the *Arrow* sailed to the Pearl River headed for Canton, the Chinese coastguard intercepted it and detained the twelve-man Chinese crew. At the time the British consul in Canton, Rutherford Alcock, was absent and was represented by Harry Parkes as acting consul. Parkes had travelled to England in 1841 to work there as a translator. That year he was appointed first secretary and translator to Sir Henry Pottinger, the British plenipotentiary for trade with China.

With the First Opium War having already broken out, Parkes quickly became involved in the hostilities. He changed positions to work as translator for Alcock in Fuzhou and survived an attack by stone-throwing Chinese soldiers. This coincided with negotiations with the provincial government over restitution for damages that a local revolt had caused to British property in the port city. In 1848 Parkes accompanied the vice consul in Shanghai to Nanjing to set the terms of punishment for Chinese who had attacked three British missionaries in Qingpu. After a period back in Britain Parkes began work in 1851 as an interpreter in the port city of Amoy. That same year he was transferred to Canton and, as British consul in Canton, was again sent to Amoy. After negotiating a treaty between Britain and

Siam in 1855 Parkes returned to Canton, where he became involved in the Arrow Incident.

Parkes had remained in close contact with the Chinese for years and was thoroughly versed in Sino-British relations. He spoke fluent Chinese (and Japanese) and regularly communicated with the Chinese governor-general of Canton, Ye Mingchen. The outbreak of the Second Opium War resulted from deliberate British manipulation of an incident that could have been resolved with far less effort – had the British side not been looking for an excuse to commence hostilities and pursue its interests in China even more intensively.

After the Chinese crew of the *Arrow* had been arrested, Parkes sent the Chinese governor-general a letter of protest, pointing out that the hauling in of the British flag by Chinese troops constituted an insult. Ye Mingchen replied that the *Arrow* was Chinese-owned and was not even flying the British flag at the time. Parkes then reported the incident to the British governor of Hong Kong, Sir John Bowring, portraying it as a violation of the rights guaranteed to the British by the Treaty of Nanjing, including respect for the British flag. As Ye Mingchen refused to apologize or make amendments, on 29 October 1856 the Royal Navy bombarded the city walls of Canton. Parkes entered the city with the commanding admiral and occupied Ye Mingchen's office building. Soon afterwards Chinese forces torched European representations outside Canton. As the available British forces were inadequate to permanently occupy Canton, they retreated. Reinforcements for the main campaign arrived in November 1857. The British also secured the support of France, the u.s. and Russia. Only the French, however, were willing to send troops.

The death of a French missionary, Auguste Chapdelaine, gave the French a plausible reason to take up arms. Born in La-Rochelle-Normande in 1814, Chapdelaine came to China in 1852. Two years later, in December 1854, he was arrested within days of arriving in a small town in Guangxi province, where he and some 300 Chinese converts celebrated a Catholic mass. He was released three weeks later and left the region after receiving threats. Only a year later did he return to Guangxi. There he was reported by a relative of a newly converted Chinese person, arrested, severely beaten and then locked inside an iron cage that hung at the entrance to the local prison. He died inside the cage and was posthumously beheaded. In 2000 Pope John Paul II canonized Chapdelaine, together with Chinese martyrs who had been killed because of their faith.

Chapdelaine's fate caused the outrage required in France for that country to support the British in the Second Opium War, as it became known. In 1857 the allied troops took Canton without notable resistance. They were helped by the civil war in the country that tied up the government's forces. The campaign was set in motion on 12 December 1857 by a delegation that issued an ultimatum to the officials of the governor-general of Canton. When no response was forthcoming, the British commenced bombarding Canton on 28 December. The next day they breached the city walls. On 5 January reinforced units penetrated inside the city. Parkes personally led a unit of marines who took Ye Mingchen prisoner. Four days later, on 9 January, the Chinese consul was reinstated to his office, but actual power rested with two Europeans, Parkes and a French marine officer. As only Parkes could speak Chinese, the administration of Canton was effectively solely in his hands. The two European states established a court, founded a police unit and opened the port on 10 February, thereby attaining the first goal of the campaign.

After the opening of Canton the British and French forces moved north, taking the Dagu Forts near Tianjin in 1858. During preparations to march on the capital, Beijing, the Chinese side dispatched negotiators who eventually produced the Treaty of Tianjin, in which the U.S. and Russia were also included. The treaty's key provision was the opening of (initially) ten additional 'treaty ports' to foreign trade. The Treaty of Nanjing, the first 'Unequal Treaty' that ended the First Opium War, had secured the opening of five ports – Fuzhou, Canton, Ningbo, Shanghai and Amoy – to trade with foreigners. Now, after the Second Opium War, this second Unequal Treaty created ten additional treaty ports, including Nanjing on the mainland and Taiwan.

When hunting pirates, British ships would now be permitted to enter any Chinese port. Foreigners' freedom of movement was extended to within a 50-km radius of each treaty port. And finally, from the British viewpoint, the Chinese government legalized the importation of opium under the irrelevant conditions that it be sold exclusively in port areas and with a certain import tariff included in the price.

The British also made sure that their standard weights and measures would be used in the ports and customs offices, and that English was introduced as the official language of commerce. Insulting or condescending characterizations of the British would be banned in Chinese documents. Diplomatic relations were officially established and Christian missionary work permitted without restrictions. A large financial indemnity paid to Britain and France rounded off the treaty's terms.[10] The British pledged in return to pull their troops out of Tianjin and evacuate the destroyed Dagu Forts.

For a time the Chinese government refused to ratify the document, after which the British and their French allies again bombarded the Dagu Forts. The Chinese resistance was stiffer than expected and caused heavy casualties among the allied troops, making reinforcements necessary. A British-Indian force of 11,000 and 6,700 French troops assembled at Hong Kong and sailed north. On 1 August they landed near Peitang. The fortifications there had been abandoned and the force advanced on the Dagu Forts.

Parkes led the capitulation talks with the quickly defeated Chinese in Dagu and, on 24 August, reached Tianjin, where he opened talks with Chinese representatives. When it became clear that these did not have the expected authority of the emperor, the allied troops continued their advance. Parkes raced ahead of them to negotiate with the authorities in Tongzhou. The two sides agreed to meet in an area where the British were to set up their camp, about 8 km outside the city. Parkes had himself led to the spot and saw that, in violation of the just-agreed terms, Chinese troops were assembling there. A second round of talks in Tongzhou ended without result and Parkes set out to return to the British headquarters with his delegation.

Although the group flew the appropriate flags to identify itself as a negotiating team, it was captured and taken to the Manchu general, who ordered Parkes, a private secretary of Lord Elgin called Henry Loch and three others (two Frenchmen and a Sikh) to be handed over to Beijing. There they were brought before a criminal court, placed in shackles and tortured. Several days later, one of the emperor's sons, a Prince Gong, had Parkes and Loch taken to more comfortable quarters. There he pressured them to support Chinese interests among the British commanders. Parkes refused to make any pledges. On 8 October the Chinese set Parkes free. The emperor's order to execute him and his delegation arrived shortly afterwards, too late. The Chinese placed a large bounty on his capture but there would be no more opportunities. Parkes took part in other campaigns in China and in talks with the Taiping rebels. He ended his career in Japan, where he survived several assassination attempts after drawing the ire of conservative elements for uncompromisingly supporting reformers during the Meiji Period.

After Parkes's fortunate release the allied forces advanced on Beijing, which they captured on 6 October. Ever since the Treaty of Tianjin had been signed, a corps of 30 British and French envoys had been stationed in the Chinese capital to pave the way for the establishment of diplomatic relations. Emperor Xianfeng ordered that these men should also be arrested and tortured. Thirteen Britons and seven French were killed. This atrocity prompted the Anglo-French force to move on the Old Summer Palace northeast of Beijing. The British commander, Lord Elgin, ordered that one of the biggest and most impressive complexes of buildings from China's later imperial period be pillaged and then razed to the ground.

Construction of the complex had begun in 1709. All subsequent emperors had expanded the site. Their designs were the first example of attempts to blend European and Chinese design elements on an increasingly vast scale. At its peak the palace consisted of 140 buildings on 350 hectares (more than 860 acres). Inspiration had come from the Jesuit priests, the painter Castiglione and other European scientists and artists who stayed in Beijing over the shorter or longer term. Exquisite gardens and an extraordinarily well-endowed library were attached to this huge complex. The destruction wrought by Elgin's troops and the irretrievable loss of cultural treasures cannot be adequately described in words. One notable fact was that the French co-commander General Montauban, disgusted by what he saw, refused to take part in the orgy of destruction.

As a trophy from his plunder, Elgin returned to Britain the precious clocks that Lord Macartney had given to the Emperor Qianlong as a gift from George III. The extent of public approval of this utterly imperialist war was shown by the name of the Pekinese dog presented as a gift to Queen Victoria from an officer who, having found it running stray in the Summer Palace, surmised it had been the emperor's lapdog. Delighted, the queen accepted the gift and named the animal 'Looty'.[11]

The Chinese Emperor Xianfeng had fled north ahead of Elgin's advancing forces. There he had little choice but to agree to the new peace conditions. The British had taken advantage of China's helpless position to expand the 'Convention of Beijing' from 18 October 1860 to include the opening of an eleventh treaty port, Tianjin, additional war reparations payments and territorial concessions in favour of Britain on the Kowloon Peninsula. The British and French secured the right to use Chinese workers in their colonies. The reparations, previously totalling 6 million taels, were expanded to 8 million silver taels each for Britain and France. When the Chinese consented to these conditions, the British and French pulled out of Beijing.[12]

Eight years later, voices were raised in Britain that sought to place the country's dealings with China on more equitable foundations. A British emissary, Rutherford Alcock, negotiated a modification of the 1858 treaty with the Chinese. Yet Parliament saw little sense in such gestures and refused to approve the text.

EIGHT

The Russian Intervention: *Trauma 3*

IN 1689 CHINA'S Qing Empire signed the Treaty of Nerchinsk (Treaty of Nipchu in Chinese) with the Tsarist Empire to fix the borders between the two states. Cossacks began crossing the Urals in 1581, especially those under the leader Yermak, who, with fewer than 1,000 Cossacks and mercenaries, gradually pushed eastward, colonizing regions inhabited by numerous Siberian nomadic peoples. Whereas the French had to cross the Mediterranean to Algeria to add colonies to their homelands, and the British entire oceans to North America and Nigeria, Russia merely had to surmount the Urals, the natural frontier to the territories beyond.

By the mid-seventeenth century the Cossacks had reached the Sea of Okhotsk. Soon the Russians in the East encountered the Han Chinese, who were incrementally expanding to the south, west and north. Both empires met up on foreign – that is, forcibly occupied – territory. The indigenous nomadic tribes were as powerless against the Tsarist forces as they were against the advancing troops and administrative structures of the Han Chinese, who initially wanted only tribute payments and occasional plunder, and considered their western frontiers as a kind of glacis. Still, the Treaty of Nerchinsk could only delay direct confrontation between China and Russia.

Since the 1840s the increasingly apparent feebleness of the Chinese, caused by domestic uprisings and the aggression of the Europeans along parts of the eastern coast, gave the Russians enough reason to resume their advance into regions claimed by the Chinese in the west. The lower reaches of the River Amur (Heilongjiang in Chinese) and Sakhalin Island were tempting prizes for the Russians. The Chinese forces, already engaged in the Second Opium War, were in no position to oppose Russia.

Under threat of war, in 1858 the Chinese governor of the region of Heilongjiang signed the Russian-Chinese Treaty of Aigun. China was forced to accept huge territorial losses south of the Outer Hinggan Range and north of the Amur totalling more than 600,000 sq. km. Another region of 400,000 sq. km. east of the Wusuli River was placed under the 'joint control' of Russia and China. But the Russian invaders were half-satisfied only once they had taken control of the port the Chinese knew as Haishenwei. The goal of the Russian campaign was expressed in the name they gave to their new settlement: Vladivostok, or 'rule in the east.'

Only two years later, in 1860, Russia took advantage of China's vulnerability at the very moment that Anglo-French troops were advancing on Beijing. Threatening war, in the Treaty of Beijing the Russians forced the Chinese to cede full control of the huge 'jointly controlled' territories east of the Wusuli. Four years later, the Tsarists wanted more. In 1864 the Chinese government was forced to sign the Protocol of Chunguchak, which gave the Russians control of 440,000 more square km of previously Chinese-occupied territory south and east of Lake Balkhash. The preliminary conclusion of agreements between China and Russia was the Treaty of St Petersburg in 1881, which fixed the Amur and Ussuri rivers as the (by no means undisputed) border between the two great empires.

NINE

The French Intervention: *Trauma 4*

FRANCE HAD JOINED Great Britain in using the conflict that later became known as the Second Opium War to expand its influence in China. French missionaries, and later the French Republic, had established a presence in Southeast Asia and built up a colonial realm called French Indochina without interference from other European powers.

Before the arrival of the Europeans this land, which has been known as Vietnam since the end of the Second World War, had had an eventful, 2,000-year history marked politically by two main factors.[13] First, domestic political upheavals and conflicts with its western neighbours, especially Siam and Burma, ensured frequent changes in dynasties and rulers. Second, the land's gigantic northern neighbour left no opportunity unused to advance its territorial expansion in this region as well.

Three times the Chinese managed to incorporate the territory for extended periods. Each time, however, the 'Vietnamese' succeeded in throwing off the imperial yoke, to focus again on their own internal political disputes and conflicts with the western neighbours. They escaped the subsequent fate of Tibet and the Uighurs of becoming permanently integrated into the Chinese state and subordinated to Han culture. When the French appeared in the region, 'Vietnam' was independent, but China still considered the central part, Annam, a tributary state.

The first period of Chinese domination of the Vietnamese lands began during the early Han Dynasty. The exact origins of Chinese influence are unclear. What we do know is that in 111 BCE a Han army defeated the 'Southern Yue', Nam Viet in the local language, and ruled there for the following 150 years. The Chinese not only levied taxes on the population, but established large agricultural entities there and imported Chinese farmers to tend them. Chinese bureaucrats quickly replaced the indigenous elites. Willing members of the local population were also drafted into service. All aspects of Chinese culture were exported to Vietnam, yet in the long run, complete integration proved unattainable.

One reason was that although the Vietnamese were no match for the advancing Chinese both militarily and numerically, they were a nation with their own long-established culture and literature, and therefore a profound sense of themselves. Their relatively mild treatment at the hands of the occupiers in the first century after the invasion did nothing to change this. When the cultural and political pressure later increased, the indigenous people rebelled and pushed the Chinese out of their country. Here, one additional factor played a decisive role.

Vietnamese culture, together with several others along China's southeastern margins, had strong matriarchal elements. The Chinese had difficulties understanding the resulting structures. They were accustomed to training men in their administrative systems and then using them in ways to suit Chinese political interests. The invaders never hesitated to integrate young men from colonized foreign nations into their civil service, thereby binding the various ethnic groups more closely within the empire. To set this process in motion in Vietnam, the Chinese changed marital laws with the aim of building up a patriarchal society. Of course, this attempt was thoroughly naive. Changes as profound as the replacement of female with male dominance cannot be effected by administrative decree. Unsurprisingly, two women initiated the revolts that helped end the first era of Chinese dominance. A nobleman's widow whose husband had been killed by a Vietnamese collaborator with the Chinese headed the national uprising with her sister. Its armies drove the Chinese out of the country; the two women were installed as the monarchs of the liberated country.

That freedom did not last long. Only three years later, in 43 CE, the Chinese invaded again, and this time they had apparently learned from their mistakes. Chinese governors led the administration. Even the collapse of the Han Dynasty in the early third century did not weaken the Chinese hold on Vietnam. Once again it was a woman who, in 245, briefly interrupted the Chinese regime: Bà Triệu. Yet she could not hold power long. Only in 544 did the second period of Chinese ascendency in Vietnam end, when internal conflict weakened the regime and a Vietnamese bureaucrat, Lý Bí, grasped the opportunity. He assembled armed forces on land and sea under his command and pushed the Chinese out; to demonstrate that he was the equal of his mighty northern neighbour he was proclaimed the first emperor of a country that received the name Van Xuan, or 'eternal spring.'

The Chinese did not keep their distance. That same year, the newly established Liang Dynasty sent a huge army of 110,000 men to change matters to their advantage. Fighting with the defenders continued with varying fortunes until 550, when the Vietnamese inflicted decisive defeats on the Chinese that led to the invaders' complete withdrawal.

About half a century later, the Sui Dynasty mounted a third attempt to permanently subjugate Vietnam. From 602 to 618 the Sui and later the Tang dynasties held onto a limited region in the north of the country, corresponding approximately with the city of Hanoi today. The more southerly region of Annam came under looser Chinese rule. There the Chinese governors were extras rather than protagonists; power remained in the hands of indigenous rulers. Yet the Chinese demonstrated their resolve in the aftermath of an uprising which took place between 722 and 728. Charged with reestablishing order, a Chinese eunuch general resolved to teach the Vietnamese a lesson they would not forget. He ordered that 80,000 Vietnamese rebels be decapitated, their bodies skinned, their heads scalped and the corpses piled into pyramids visible for great distances.[14] In 906 a local ruler in Annam managed to shake off Tang rule. He entered into an agreement with the Chinese, who then recognized him as the first regent in Vietnam.

Five hundred years passed before a fourth and, to date, final attempt was made to bring Vietnam under Chinese control. In 1407 the forces of the Ming Dynasty occupied the country and introduced a period of forced cultural hegemony. Important elements of cultural identification were plundered and destroyed; the classical Vietnamese canon was banned in favour of Chinese literature. Yet time was not on the Chinese side. Mounting signs of the Ming Dynasty's inner decay sparked several nationalist revolts that liberated the country as early as 1427. Founded by a general in 1428, the dynasty remained nominally in power until the end of the eighteenth century, even if after some time the rulers were only considered puppets of the leading families in the northern (Tonkin) and southern (Cochinchina) parts of the country.

After a rebellion in the south forced the Nguyen family from power, a French Catholic missionary, Pigneau de Behaine, proved to be a saviour, if not a selfless one. Pierre Joseph Georges Pigneau arrived in southern Vietnam in 1767.[15] Ten years later, nearly the entire Nguyen family had been wiped out. A surviving fifteen-year-old prince named Nguyen Anh found refuge at Pigneau's mission. In the time that followed, the missionary repeatedly rescued the young man from the grasp of his pursuers, joined him on adventurous escapes, assisted him in his military attempts to regain power and shared his defeats. Finally, Nguyen Anh entrusted his son Nguyen Phuc Canh to Pigneau's care. The missionary travelled with the boy, making several stops and requesting military and financial assistance before arriving at the court of Louis XVI.

In 1787 the French king and Nguyen Anh signed the Treaty of Versailles. That date marked the beginning of French Indochina. In return for supporting the Vietnamese pretender to the throne in his efforts to retake power, Nguyen Anh gave the French the island of Pulo Condore, where the British East India Company had maintained a base since 1702. The French later used the place as a prison island (as did the United States during the Vietnam War). France also received exclusive trading rights in the port city of Da Nang in Annam, the central part of Vietnam.

Despite these advances, the stubborn missionary endured further setbacks, not least because of the revolution in France and substantial opposition within Church ranks to his overtly political approach to his work. In 1789 he had, after all, organized a motley army at the French base at Pondicherry in southern India that had indeed put Nguyen Anh back on the throne. As Emperor Gia Long, Nguyen ruled all three parts of the country – Tonkin, Annam and Cochinchina.

In reward for his efforts Pigneau hoped the Catholic Church would be permitted to redouble its missionary activities in the region and expand the French presence in Southeast Asia, especially since the British had seen such enormous success in India. His second wish was certainly granted, but his missionary hopes would be disappointed. Prince Canh was meant to become Vietnam's first Catholic monarch, but the royal heir's early death put an end to such plans.

Da Nang, which the French had already opened as a result of the Treaty of Versailles, rapidly grew into an important hub for Asian–European trade. Yet the situation remained unsatisfactory for the French. In 1847 the persecution of French missionaries provided a pretext for sabre-rattling. French warships entered the port and bombarded the city. Eleven years later, again in response to attacks on French missionaries, Emperor Napoleon III ordered another military expedition that was initially successful but retreated in 1860 after facing stiff Vietnamese resistance. The French then took Saigon, and two years later put two southern provinces under their control. The Treaty of Saigon, which the Vietnamese government was forced to accept after a peasant revolt in the north, awarded the French reparations, permitted missionary activities, opened the Mekong River to French shipping and confirmed French rule in large parts of Cochinchina, the most southerly section of the country's long coastline.

The French soon recognized, however, that the Red River was more important than the Mekong as a gateway to China. Therefore in 1872 they invaded the Tonkin region, pulling their troops out only when, on 15 March 1874, another treaty opened the Red River to French commerce and confirmed French power in the south. When it became known that the Vietnamese government had also committed to coordinating its foreign policy with France, a rebellion broke out all over the country, prompting yet another big French military campaign. A preliminary treaty in 1883 and a final one in 1884 sealed Vietnam's future as a French protectorate.

The loss of Vietnam's sovereignty to France was another trauma for China against which it had no defence. Chinese attempts to subjugate their southern neighbours had not resumed since the withdrawal of Chinese forces in 1427, yet later Vietnamese rulers were well advised to duly pay their tributes to China. The establishment of a French protectorate of Indochina ended the admittedly formal inclusion of Vietnam in the Chinese sphere of influence and would cause the direct clash of French and Chinese claims along what from then on was a mutual border.

TEN

The Japanese Intervention: *Trauma 5*

JAPAN IS AN ISLAND chain northeast of China. Since the second half of the first millennium CE the two countries' cultures have remained closely linked, not least through the Korean Peninsula that lies between them. Many elements of Chinese culture found their way to Japan, were adopted there and, often enough, were further refined according to demanding aesthetic and contextual standards. Japanese writing, music, architecture and medicine are the most prominent examples, the latter based largely on the *Nanjing*, a Chinese work on the theory and practice of medicine from about the first century CE, and the *Shanghan lun*, a collection of remedies from the author-physician Zhang Ji (*c.* 200 CE). To this day, Japanese call the discipline of preparing remedies derived from this book *kanpo*, or '(Han-)Chinese recipes'. Confucianism, and especially the neo-Confucianism that followed the Song Dynasty, landed on fertile soil in Japan. Buddhism, the faith besides Shintoism – an indigenous form of animism – that is most widespread in Japan, also arrived in the islands from China. The sociologist Max Weber went so far as to call Japan a 'moonlight culture' – one that shines not by its own light, but by reflecting that of the Chinese sun.

Irrespective of its tight cultural bonds with the Chinese mainland, Japan always stayed politically independent. The epic attempts of Kublai Khan, already discussed, to include Japan in his empire foundered as much on the fierce resistance of the Japanese defenders as on luck or, as the Japanese believed, the divine intercession of two powerful storms. The Japanese overlords might never have come upon the idea of leaving their island realm to hazard an invasion of China and take for themselves the mother soil of much of their own civilization. Yet the manifest decline of the Manchu Empire during the nineteenth century did not only tempt the Europeans to grab ever bigger shares of the Chinese spoils that were practically there for the taking. The empire of Japan likewise sensed its chance to aggrandize itself by emulating the British, French and others.

This emulation must have seemed all the more auspicious to the Japanese, as they had already introduced a reform process during the 1860s that, for China, still lay far in the future. Since China's cultural self-image was still largely intact in the mid-nineteenth century, abandoning it was out of the question. It was a painful process for the Japanese that had to be pushed through in the teeth of constant opposition from nationalist conservatives. Without the protagonists being aware of it at the time, the reforms in Japan were ultimately that country's act of exchanging Chinese cultural hegemony for that of Europe. One skin was partially discarded and another donned in its stead.

Japan first appeared on the horizons of Europe's expanding concerns in the sixteenth century, when Portuguese missionaries first attempted to make Japan a colony of Catholicism. In fact they made substantial progress, also attracting other Catholic groups who promptly began to clash over the willing Japanese converts. The Thirty Years War in Europe, characterized at least superficially by rival sectarian camps, cast its shadow all the way to the Far East, however. Japanese leaders decided to clamp down, lest the armed European conflict over interpreting the Gospels that they were hearing about spilled over to their own country with the same appalling results.

The Christians had had their chance. Their joyous tidings had even been welcomed for a time. However, since they had failed – both in Central Europe and in Asia – to act with the peace and goodwill that their own teachings required, in 1612 the Japanese government issued a local and in 1615 a nationwide ban on missionary work. All missionaries, most of them Spanish or Portuguese, were expelled. Japanese converts were given a choice: either to abjure their faith in a ceremony mocking an image of Christ, or be executed.

From the mid-seventeenth century, contact with other countries stopped almost completely. On the one hand, this was to keep out the missionaries. On the other, the Tokugawa Shoguns, who ruled over a feudal society with vassal structures, saw that the lucrative foreign trade that some local leaders were success-fully conducting would eventually threaten their own power. They therefore restricted foreign contacts to those with the Dutch, who professed no interest in Christian missionary work. They were permitted to keep a small trading post on the artifi-cial island of Dejima in the port of Nagasaki, with contact with the outside world sometimes limited to one ship per year. This tiny outpost, which the authorities would always regard with suspicion, nonetheless drew the interest of more than a handful of Japanese and would eventually become Western science's gateway to Japan. Called 'Dutch studies' or *rangaku*, elements of European scientific culture, notably the natural sciences and medicine, spread (legally or otherwise) from Dejima into Japanese society. At first only those men selected to be inter-preters, but subsequently also doctors and experts in other fields, developed an interest in the therapies, military technol-ogy, agricultural knowledge and even political theories of the Dutch, who responded by supplying more books either written in or translated into Dutch.

The merchants based on Dejima were also joined by scholars who were determined to find out as much about Japan as they possibly could. From 1690 to 1692, for example, a German scientist named Engelbert Kaempfer used his position as a doctor on Dejima to collect Japanese books, animals, plants and many more specimens during his few authorized travels to the mainland, and take them back to Europe with him. He did so with the secret collaboration of his interpreter and other Japan-ese scholars.

Another German who found his way to Dejima and worked there from 1823 to 1829 and again from 1859 to 1862 was the Bavarian physician and researcher Philipp Franz von Siebold. He came to Japan at a time when the Europeans on Dejima had been permitted far more freedom of movement than they had in Kaempfer's day. Siebold took a Japanese wife with whom he fathered a daughter; he also enjoyed the trust of Japanese doctors and scholars, and even of political leaders. He was regularly allowed to explore the country, and to establish a school where he taught the pupils various European fields of knowledge in Dutch. Only his Japanese interpreter, who spoke Dutch better than Siebold did, knew that he was not really a Dutchman.

Siebold's European medical training also gave him frequent access to prominent patients at the highest levels of Japanese society. He made it a principle not to accept payment for his treatments, which included Japan's first cowpox vaccination. Instead the Japanese gave him precious gifts. Siebold accepted only those with scientific or ethnological value, and in this way amassed an extensive collection that would later earn him the sobriquet 'scientific discoverer of Japan'.

The esteem in which Siebold is held to this day overlooks the darker side of his collector's impulse. He could never resist the temptation of hoodwinking his generous hosts and recklessly exposing them to danger. In one unfortunate incident, in which his vessel was shipwrecked on the Japanese coast as he was leaving the country, the cargo was recovered and found to include geographical maps of Japan, which laws strictly forbade to be taken out of the country. Several of his Japanese confidantes were subsequently executed; others received prison sentences. Siebold himself was forbidden to re-enter Japan. Three decades later, that ban became superfluous after the virtual wall that the Tokugawa shoguns had erected around Japan collapsed.

After almost 270 years, domestic political turbulence brought the country's feudal system to its limits. Power structures shifted; several revolts eroded the Tokugawa's monopoly on power. The time was ripe for those forces that sought to open Japan to global trade – and their own interests – further than the tiny Dutch establishment in Nagasaki harbour permitted.

Unintentionally brought onto the scene by the Dutch, the u.s. soon moved into the foreground. Between 1789 and 1809 the Netherlands could no longer send ships to the Far East because of the Napoleonic Wars, so the country invited the Americans to trade in Nagasaki under the Dutch flag. Themselves occupiers of a land whose first nations had either been killed in conflicts with the European invaders or banished to largely miserable existences on reservations, the Americans soon began extending their feelers in various directions beyond the part of the North American continent that had become theirs.

The first achievement – the annexation of Alaska – was completely bloodless. This gigantic territory of more than 1.7 million sq. km belonged until 1867 to Tsarist Russia, the government of which regarded the distant possession as more of a burden than an asset. The territory was difficult to reach, the trade in furs weakened through overhunting and the indigenous peoples were always resisting Russian administration. The Tsar also needed money to pay the costs of the Crimean War, so in 1867 a treaty was signed that sold the territory to the United States for $7.2 million. In the U.S. the purchase was anything but universally welcomed, but policymakers who saw long-term gains for the country by acquiring Alaska won the day. Their efforts would later benefit the country enormously.

In 1898 the U.S. annexed the Hawaiian Islands; soon afterwards U.S. troops drove the Spanish out of the Philippines, putting Japan into a vice-like grip in the north from Alaska, east through Hawaii and in the south by occupying the Philippines. The U.S. also captured Guam Island that year, further extending America's presence in the western Pacific. In 1899 the western part of the Samoan Islands also came under U.S. rule. Policy towards Japan fitted these expansionist efforts.

Independent attempts by U.S. economic interests – aided by warships – failed in 1837 and 1846 to establish contact with the Japanese through Nagasaki. Only in 1849 did a U.S. captain, James Glynn, succeed in negotiating directly with Japanese authorities in Nagasaki harbour. After his return he advised Congress to open up Japan, if necessary by a show of strength.

It seemed that the right man to do the 'prying' was Commodore Matthew Perry. The naval officer prepared intensively for his mission. A sizeable literature already existed about the closed country, and Perry even consulted with Philipp Franz von Siebold, who after his unfortunate departure from Japan was living in the Dutch city of Leyden. Well informed and accompanied by four menacing black warships, Perry sailed in 1852 from Norfolk, Virginia, reaching the harbour of Uraga, near present-day Tokyo, which was known at the time as Edo, the following July. The Japanese immediately demanded that the squadron move on to Nagasaki, still the country's only port open to foreigners. Perry refused, steamed past the Japanese ships and trained his guns on the city of Uraga. He issued an ultimatum demanding that the Japanese withdraw their ships or see them destroyed, and that they give him an opportunity to hand over a letter from u.s. president Millard Fillmore. The Japanese said they would accept the letter in the harbour of Kurihama. Perry acted accordingly, then left Japanese waters with his fleet, saying that he would return and expect a reply. After the flotilla was gone, the Japanese began fortifying Tokyo Bay against a possible u.s. attack.

In February 1854 Perry returned to Japan, this time with eight warships and, to his surprise, received an offer for a treaty that fulfilled almost all his demands. On 31 March Perry signed the Convention of Kanagawa, which secured the opening of two additional ports, Shimoda and Hakodate, to trade with the Americans. The Japanese side also guaranteed shelter for ship-wrecked American whalers and permitted the establishment of a u.s. consulate. Perry had succeeded in ending Japan's self-imposed isolation. Russia and the British received similar privileges soon afterwards. Only four years later, in 1858, the Japanese and the u.s. signed a 'treaty of amity and commerce', the terms of which included extraterritoriality for u.s. nationals in Japan and low import tariffs for u.s. goods.

After fulfilling his mission in Japan, Perry sailed for the southern Chinese island of Taiwan, where he explored possibilities for coal-mining. After returning to the u.s. he recommended Taiwan as an easily defensible base for additional operations in the Far East, comparing it with the role that Cuba had played for the Spanish in the New World. Perry also pointed out that holding Taiwan could break the European monopoly on trade routes to the region. The project never materialized, however, because President Franklin Pierce turned down Perry's recommendations, saying that such a distant possession would be a waste of money that Congress would never approve anyway.

Thanks to its long-lasting contacts with the Dutch and other Europeans through the port of Nagasaki, Japan was not unprepared for the encounters with European culture that from then on would expand continually. Yet internal problems and the capitulation to the u.s. demands, as abrupt as it was humiliating, led rapidly to the end of both the Tokugawa Shogunate and a political culture that recalled the situation before the Edo period that sought mainly to avoid the threat of colonization.

Despite intermittent disturbances in its early years opposing what was considered by some to be excessive westernization, the Meiji Reform Period that began in 1868 introduced a far-reaching programme of modernization to Japan. Scouts were sent to many European countries to determine the strengths of these nations, and then invite instructors from whom the Japanese could quickly learn the technologies and practices deemed essential for Japan's modernization. In the space of only a few decades Japan had gained such a big advantage over its East Asian neighbours in technology and economic output that it even followed its European role models in attacking islands off the Chinese coast and, later during the twentieth century, attempting to colonize great stretches of territory on the mainland.

Taiwan, the island dismissed by the u.s. president, was the first target of aggressive Japanese colonization at China's expense in the nineteenth century. Ever since the first landing was made in 1592, Taiwan had repeatedly been the destination of Japanese military expeditions. At that time the population was already mixed. The majority of the inhabitants, with Malay or Micronesian roots, faced a small minority of ethnic Chinese who had come from the nearby mainland.

The first Europeans to land on the island were the Portuguese in 1583, who named the place Formosa – a term that remained widely used in Europe until the late twentieth century. Four decades later, the Spanish and the Dutch East India Company gained footholds on the island's southern end. The Dutch needed workers and imported large numbers of mainland

Chinese. Within a few decades they had extended their author-ity to about two-thirds of the mountainous island, but were driven out again in the mid-seventeenth century by Chinese forces loyal to the recently deposed Ming Dynasty that had fled there. In 1683 the Manchu Dynasty also invaded Taiwan and claimed it from then on as Chinese territory. Several Japanese attempts to take the island failed.

Early in the 1870s, a conflict broke out with a shipwrecked crew from the Ryukyu Kingdom, which the Japanese considered their own. The conflict involved not only local authorities but the government in Beijing, from whom the Japanese then demanded compensation. When none was forthcoming, 3,000 Japanese troops landed on Taiwan; the Chinese government followed with its own force soon afterwards. Yet no real fighting broke out. The confrontation with China took place in another location that was much more favourable to the Japanese, namely Korea.

In the nineteenth century Korea was a kingdom required to pay tribute to China but otherwise largely independent. Japan's Meiji reforms included extending the country's sphere of influ-ence on the peninsula, coming up against both Russia and China in the process. The Korean population was divided, with one part favouring keeping the old order and orientation toward China and the other preferring rapid modernization. This faction naturally looked more to Japan, which had already introduced its reform programme. By 1894 a series of revolts by reformers had finally threatened the survival of the government in Seoul, which was no longer able to stand up to the reformers on its own. It called for Chinese help. The Qing Dynasty sent 3,000 troops and informed Japan on the basis of the 1885 Treaty of Tianjin. Japan also sent a force to protect its interests.

The first fighting took place in June 1894. Four Japanese cruisers started a battle with three Chinese warships, only one of which survived the duel. The Japanese occupied the palace in Seoul and installed a new, pro-Japanese government. On 1 August the Japanese formally declared war. After several battles on land and at sea, all of which ended in defeat and sometimes utter destruction for the Chinese, by the spring of 1895 and eight months of fighting the Chinese had recognized their defeat and accepted capitulation talks, which were completed on 17 April 1895 with the signing of the Treaty of Shimonoseki.

Japan received Taiwan, the nearby Pescadores Islands and the Liaodong Peninsula in northern China. The Chinese were also forced to pay the enormous sum of 7.45 million kg of silver to Japan as reparations. The huge burden that paying this amount represented for China becomes apparent when one considers that China's annual tax revenue equalled less than half the sum. Japan also received the right to use Chinese trade ports and could export rice without import tariffs to China at a big profit. Two years later the Japanese parliament debated selling Taiwan to France, but the proposal was dropped. From then on Japan continued its efforts to establish complete control over the island. While the Chinese population on the coastal plains was forced into loyalty with a combination of carrots and sticks, the non-Chinese peoples who had been increasingly pushed back into the remote interior remained recalcitrant. Even ruthless military campaigns accomplished little.

After the Treaty of Shimonoseki and following an intervention of France, Germany and Russia, Russia received the right to lease the Liaodong Peninsula in a subsequent treaty. That experience left the Japanese embittered, and after fighting a victorious war with Russia in 1904–05, Japan regained the strategically important peninsula in the Treaty of Portsmouth. In much the same way that European colonialism was driven by economic theories that regarded economic survival as safe-guarded only by global expansion of both trade and the self-determined access to both resources and markets, the Japanese government, prompted not least by fast industrialization and the doubling of the country's population to 52 million between the beginning of the Meiji reforms and 1913, considered it-self both justified and compelled to secure raw materials and penetrate new markets beyond the home islands.[16]

ELEVEN

The German Intervention: *Trauma 6*

AS THE BRITISH were extending their dominions in India and then led the grab for China, France focused on its holdings in Indochina and the Russian Empire pushed into China from the north. During this time there was no Germany yet that could have joined this movement of European powers, which also included Portugal, Spain and the Netherlands among its active protagonists. Prussia followed global politics attentively and waited for an opportunity to catch up. The economic theory that overseas colonies were essential for the prosperity of the home-land had taken hold in every European country able to devote attention to events beyond its borders. Enticed by what already seemed like China's infinite market potential, Prussia built its own East Asia squadron and sent it to the Far East in 1860.

The Bay of Kiautschou (Jiaozhou), further north than the havens of the Portuguese in Macao and the British in Hong Kong yet closer to the capital, Beijing, soon caught the Prussians' interest. Yet the time for a takeover was not yet ripe. The Prussians first signed commercial treaties with China and Japan in 1861. The pact with China required mediation by the British and French, as the Chinese saw no reason to become involved with such an insignificant country.[17] In 1868 and 1871 Ferdinand von Richthofen was sent to reconnoitre the region; he also recommended the Bay of Kiautschou as a suitable naval base.

After the founding of the German Empire in 1871 the government continued Prussia's efforts to catch up, especially with the British, in the race for colonies.

The search for a good gateway to China comparable to the British crown colony of Hong Kong continued for several years. After the Sino–Japanese Treaty of Shimonoseki in 1895 the Germans blocked the cession of Liaodong to Japan in the hope that China would return the favour by granting Germany its own commercial and military base on the mainland. When that hope went unfulfilled, German policymakers, under pressure from industrial leaders, decided to use force.

Near Shanghai north of Wusong in 1896, German cruisers steamed up the Huangpu River and anchored in the Yangtse River at Nanjing, where German military advisors had been attacked. After negotiations with local authorities had been completed and Germany's demands met, the cruiser *Prinzess Wilhelm* continued further up the river, all the way to Hangkow, where such a large, let alone foreign, ship had never before been seen. That same year Admiral Tirpitz, himself a former commander of the East Asia Squadron, inspected the Bay of Kiautschou up close; next year the Bay of Samsah on the coast of Fujian Province opposite Taiwan was also considered. Yet the final choice was Kiautschou, not least because coal could be mined in the vicinity of this secure harbour. An excuse to forcibly occupy the bay presented itself soon afterwards.[18]

Following the French Jesuits, who had been under state protection since the seventeenth century, all Roman Catholic missionaries in China were placed under French protection at the end of the eighteenth century. Therefore the first German missionaries of the Verbi Dei Society, also known as the Steyler Mission, had to enter China with French passports. Given the rivalries among European states at the time, that solution appealed neither to the missionaries nor the German authorities. Following negotiations among all concerned parties, the Vatican agreed to place the Steyler missionaries under the protection of Germany. The transfer of authority took place in June 1890. The first challenge was not long in coming.

On 1 November 1897 two Steyler missionaries, Fathers Franz Nies and Richard Henle, were attacked and killed by members of the 'Broadsword Association' (*dadaohui*) in a village called Zhangjiazhuang. The German emperor Wilhelm II used the incident as an excuse to occupy Kiautschou Bay. The Chinese government had not even been informed of the matter when the East Asia Squadron was ordered to take the bay.

German marines landed on 14 November. The Chinese made no attempts to fight back. During the ensuing negotiations the Germans refused to leave Chinese territory. While xenophobic sentiment stemming from these recurring violations of national sovereignty escalated among a Chinese population that decried these incidents as insulting, the government in Beijing again found itself unable to effectively resist the Europeans' demands. China therefore agreed to pay the costs for damage to Catholic churches and replace the German missionaries' stolen property. The churches were also to be clearly marked by plaques stating that they were protected by the Emperor of China.

The Germans also made sure that a governor who was particularly hostile to the foreigners, Li Bingheng, was demoted, with the assurance that this man would never again hold political office in which he could promote his personal beliefs. More important for the Germans, of course, were the greater aims of the talks. After issuing an ultimatum the Germans were allowed to lease an area of 552 sq. km in the Bay of Kiautschou, including large and small islands, for 99 years. Soon afterward Germany officially declared the 'German Protectorate of Kiautschou.' The Chinese side transferred authority within the leased areas to Germany.

In addition the new colonial masters were granted a concession to mine coal in the region. To transport it they demanded and received the right to build two railways. Mining was permitted within a corridor of 15 km on either side of the railway between the cities of Tsingtao and Jinan. A neutral area of 50 km around the bay was declared a buffer zone that German troops could enter freely. Any Chinese administrative activity there would have to be approved first by the Germans. The treaty was ratified on 6 March 1898.

Germany's European rivals soon followed up with their own demands for Chinese concessions. Russia received Port Arthur, while the British obtained 99-year leases on Weihai in the northeast and the 'New Territories' on the mainland side of their colony Hong Kong. Guangzhouwan, a bay in southern China, was leased to France for 99 years.

One year later the German patrons of the Steyler missionaries responded to a new challenge from the enraged local population. The incident also plainly exposed the close ties between missionaries and economic interests. While on a tour of various Christian congregations in southern Shandong Province, in November 1898 a priest named Georg M. Stenz became involved in a local disturbance apparently sparked by misdeeds of Chinese converts. The demonstrators captured and assaulted the priest, who was released only after Chinese authorities intervened two days later, and taken to Tsingtao for medical treatment.

The German Catholic bishop in Kiautschou first tried, unsuccessfully, to persuade the Chinese governor of Jinanfu to pay compensation. The next administrative level, in Rizhao, likewise refused to respond. Finally talks opened with the Chinese administrative head of South Shandong, who was basically well-disposed to the missionaries. The two sides agreed on a generous compensation payment and prosecution of all those involved in the attack on Father Stenz. In addition the bureaucrat in Rizhao was ordered to apologize solemnly. That would have been the end of the matter had the Germans not sent a punitive expedition to Rizhao in spring 1899, in which the by-then-recovered Father Stenz took an active part.

When several political parties in Germany sharply criticized the expedition, a report by the German governor of Kiautschou, Paul Jaeschke, came to its defence, saying he had 'considered the expedition necessary for purely economic reasons'.[19] The operation's purpose had been to intimidate the Chinese and help assert Germany's interests more quickly. Jaeschke's justification suggests that the colonial authorities, whether military or civilian, rather greeted the extremely provocative behaviour of some missionaries and Chinese converts. The explosions of rage among the Chinese people, who felt their traditions and customs had been deeply insulted, seem to have been welcome pretexts for the colonialists to flex their military muscle and soften the Chinese up for even more demands.[20]

TWELVE

The Boxer Protocol: *Trauma 7*

AS THE CHINESE stumbled from one military defeat to the next, and the great European powers and Japan appropriated ever-bigger chunks of the enfeebled empire's territory, each time dealing yet another blow to Chinese pride, internally the malcontents were organizing. They certainly had enough reasons. The economy was deteriorating in various parts of the country, leading to rioting. The manifest inability of the alien Manchurian regime to protect China's borders encouraged nationalists to rise up against it. When the so-called Boxer Rebellion finally broke out, the central government in Beijing managed at first to deflect the people's rage onto the imperialist powers and their alleged allies, the Chinese Christians, yet the rebellion would usher in the final phase of Qing rule over China.

The 'Righteous Fists of Harmony' (*yihuquan*, or *yihetuan*, 'Society for Righteousness and Harmony'), the Chinese name for the Boxer Rebellion which spread through northern China between 1898 and 1900, was sparked by social disturbances in Shandong province in which the 'Broadsword Society' may have been involved. Unlike the Taiping Rebellion half a century earlier, the Boxers did not produce a single charismatic leader. Local commanders encouraged the many localized revolts. Still, the protests did have something like a common platform.

The Unequal Treaties and the privileges they enshrined for foreigners, especially that of extraterritoriality, restricted Chinese sovereignty. The activities of the likewise protected Christian missionaries, who in the eyes of the Chinese meddled in local affairs that were no business of theirs, likewise stoked widespread hatred. They threatened the Confucian values of family, ancestor worship and social hierarchy, thereby endangering China's social fabric. Across the country, conservatives began staging anti-Christian demonstrations. As the Chinese word for the 'Lord' Jesus Christ (*zhu*) is a homophone of the Chinese word for pig (*zhu*), the anti-Christians frequently circulated caricatures showing a pig nailed to a cross in a Christ-like pose.

As in Japan decades before, a deep rift had opened in China between elements of the imperial court, who recognized the need for reforms, and the conservatives led by the Empress Dowager and Regent Cixi. The political conflict between these two factions effectively paralysed both the government and country politically and added to the mounting sense of crisis in China.[21]

Together with the rebels' growing willingness to use violence, an edict by the empress that some of the Boxers were law-abiding citizens set alarm bells ringing among the Europeans, Japanese and Americans, who demanded protection for their representations. A government ban on the Boxers had no effect; some imperial troops even joined the rebellion. After initial disturbances and attacks on railways with numerous casualties the foreign legations demanded military protection from their governments. The first contingent of 450 soldiers arrived in May and June 1900 in Beijing. Soon afterward a 2,000-man expeditionary force under the command of a British admiral departed Tianjin for Beijing, but was repulsed by the rebels on 26 June. The 500 Western civilians, 450 European troops and 3,000 Chinese Christians in Beijing were therefore on their own when the Boxers, crying 'Kill! Kill!', finally attacked the city's Legation Quarter.

On 3 July China attempted to win Japan over to its side in the fight against the imperialist powers. The Japanese refused, instead joining an international force that was sent to relieve the besieged garrison in Beijing. A Manchurian soldier's fatal attack on a German diplomat, Baron Clemens von Ketteler, gave the Germans the emotional grounds they needed to join the expeditionary corps. The political decision to have Germans join the fight was certainly down to the wish of the Kaiser and his advisers that Germany should finally play a major role in the alliance of great powers. A first, important success for the Germans was to see their Field Marshal Graf von Waldersee appointed the force's chief of staff. Meanwhile, the Kaiser saw off his troops in Bremerhaven with the infamous 'Hun Speech':

> A great task awaits you: you are to revenge the grievous injustice that has been done. The Chinese have overturned the law of nations; they have mocked the sacredness of the envoy, the duties of hospitality in a way unheard of in world history. It is all the more outrageous that this crime has been committed by a nation that takes pride in its ancient culture. Show the old Prussian virtue. Present yourselves as Christians in the cheerful endurance of suffering. May honour and glory follow your banners and arms. Give the whole world an example of manliness and discipline ... Should you encounter the enemy, he will be defeated! No quarter will be given! Prisoners will not be taken! Whoever falls into your hands is forfeited. Just as a thousand years ago the Huns under their King Attila made a name for themselves, one that even today makes them seem mighty in history and legend, may the name German be affirmed by you in such a way in China that no Chinese will ever again dare to look cross-eyed at a German.[22]

The emperor's choice of words went too far even for some senior German politicians, who tried unsuccessfully to prevent the speech's publication in newspapers. Equating the Germans with the Huns not only coined a rhetorical model that the British especially have been gleefully using ever since; it also incited the real atrocities that allied troops, forgetting their claim to be bringing civilization to the Chinese heathens, committed in the course of suppressing the Boxer Rebellion. In any case the reinforcements from Europe arrived too late to take part in the actual fighting. The 20,000 Anglo-Indian, Russian, Japanese and U.S. soldiers who had left Tianjin for Beijing on 4 August 1900 arrived at the Chinese capital on 13 August. Germans, Frenchmen, Austrians and Italians were involved only in small numbers without the reinforcements. Beijing was captured the following day and given over to three days of looting. Killings, pillaging and rape committed by the allied troops also accompanied the so-called punitive expeditions against the rebels' remaining bases, after the Empress Dowager had fled a safe distance on what was officially called an 'inspection trip'.[23]

Tsarist Russia used the opportunity to move 200,000 soldiers into Manchuria, ostensibly to fight rebels there. In a treaty concluded on 16 February 1901, sovereignty over the territory remained officially Chinese, but the Russian forces were authorized to remain in the region to safeguard the railways there.

Negotiations over the conditions to end the Boxer rebellion continued from October 1900 to January 1901, when the emperor's widow accepted the terms from her remote refuge in Gansu. On 7 September 1901 the Boxer Protocol, as it became known, laid down the following terms:

1 The Chinese government shall apologize for the assassination of the German Baron von Ketteler (and the Japanese embassy secretary) and erect a monument in his honour.
2 The rebels shall be punished.
3 The traditional administrative examinations shall not be held in the cities where foreigners were killed for five years.
4 China shall pay reparations totalling 1.4 billion gold marks, payable over a period of four decades.
5 Individually affected foreigners shall receive separate compensation.
6 China shall neither buy nor import arms.
7 The diplomatic quarter in Beijing shall be accessible only to foreigners and be fortified to defend against any future aggression.
8 The Dagu Forts shall be razed. Foreign military bases shall be established along the railroad between Beijing and the coast.
9 The government in Beijing shall establish a ministry of foreign affairs that shall take precedence over all other ministries of state.

10 Anti-foreign organizations shall be banned by imperial
    edict under pain of death.
11 The practice of deep bowing called kowtowing that
    violates the honour of foreign diplomatic representatives
    shall be abolished.

The full dishonour the Chinese faced was expressed in the German demand that a delegation of atonement headed by an imperial prince should be sent to Berlin to ask for forgiveness for the diplomat's killing. The Chinese barely managed to avoid the pinnacle of humiliation: having to kneel down personally in front of Kaiser Wilhelm. The atonement ceremony took place without this demeaning act on 4 September 1901 in the Grotto Room of the Neues Palais in Potsdam. Still, any observer on hand must have believed that China, the once-mighty Middle Kingdom, lay prostrate on the ground and would never recover on its own. More than a handful of Chinese people also held this opinion.

By reinforcing racism and other fear-driven intellectual currents, the pseudoscientific arguments of social Darwinism found receptive audiences beyond Europe. In China some intellectuals applied the societal variant of the survival of the fittest to relations between China and the West, and seriously believed that China would disappear from the map within decades. That was how overpowering Western technology and science – indeed, all of Western civilization – seemed. The Boxer Protocol and the Treaty of Portsmouth that ended the 1904–05 Russo–Japanese war, which was fought entirely on Chinese soil but without any Chinese participation, would be far from the last developments to nurture such pessimistic forecasts.

THIRTEEN

The Custodian Banks: *Trauma 8*

THE CHINESE EMPIRE was founded through unification under the 'first emperor of the Qin Dynasty', Qin Shi Huang Di – who remains famous to this day through the thousands of terracotta figures who accompanied him to his grave. For 2,000 years, longer than any other documented political entity in the history of civilization, the empire's structures endured until domestic decay and external challenges put it beyond the initially modest efforts of the late nineteenth and early twentieth centuries to stop its disintegration. A government that had been oblivious to contemporary reality and largely intransigent toward the necessity of reordering state and society finally admitted its defeat. On 1 January 1912 the reformers proclaimed the founding of the Chinese Republic and the last emperor, reduced to a shell of his predecessors' glory, abdicated.

An initial phase of frequent and evolving domestic political conflict lasted well into the 1920s. The main milestones of this period were the ratification of the first constitution in 1909; the proclamation of the republic under the reformer Sun Yatsen (1866–1925) two years later; the short-lived bid by the warlord Yuan Shikai (1859–1916) to re-establish the monarchy in 1915; the disturbances following the Treaty of Versailles in 1919, when the victorious powers of the First World War violated the principle of self-determination propagated by u.s. president Woodrow Wilson and handed Germany's Chinese holdings to Japan instead of returning them to China; and the gradual con-solidation of republican power throughout China in the 1920s.

A brief period of relative calm was soon followed by an increasingly violent conflict between the republicans and the Communists and the Japanese invasion, which involved simul-taneous civil war and external aggression. Only the victory of the

Communists and the founding of the People's Republic of China in 1949 brought the stability needed to start rebuilding. The reconstruction process was interrupted from the mid-1960s to the early 1970s by the convulsions of the so-called Cultural Revolution. In sum, the twentieth century marked a new beginning.

Unsurprisingly, the gigantic country's new beginning was neither swift nor without complications. Though the two millennia of imperial rule had hardly constituted a monolithic block of governance – even the final three dynasties of Yuan Mongols, Ming Chinese and Qing Manchurians had differed in numerous ways – many fundamental values remained embedded as traditions in the social hierarchies and general view of the world that, for most of China's inhabitants, had come to define their identities. Therefore the political break with the past in 1911–12 in no way completely realigned all the Chinese people. Inevitably, efforts by various regional forces and individuals to gain power would also contribute to the great upheavals of the following years and decades.

Among foreign observers and representatives of the imperialist powers' interests, uncertainty was great over what political structures might emerge from the 1911 revolution in the new republic. China had been burdened with crippling obligations in the recently signed treaties and, given the ongoing power struggles in the new state, the foreign powers were unsure whether the financial payments they had contractually secured would still be honoured. The Imperial Maritime Customs Service (IMCS) provided the leverage needed to ensure that the funds did not flow into the wrong hands (from the creditors' viewpoint).

In the second half of the nineteenth century pressure from the imperialist powers succeeded in bringing three Chinese government administrations under the de facto control of foreign interests: the Maritime Customs Service, Postal Service and Salt Service. Robert Hart (1835–1911), a Briton, served as IMCS inspector-general from 1863 to 1908. In 1898 the British secured an agreement that the service would remain in British hands as long as Great Britain remained China's most important trading partner. Although Hart always insisted that he was an official of the Chinese government, in the course of his tenure he established for himself a nearly unassailable position of power. If, at the beginning, it appeared that the revenues of the IMCS went mainly into Chinese state coffers, by 1898 China was receiving none of the proceeds at all. All customs revenues were by then being used to repay the monies that foreign lenders had lent China for the war against Japan and the subsequent reparations required by the Treaty of Shimonoseki.

The Maritime Customs Service's core tasks included suppressing smuggling, monitoring cargoes and calculating customs duties for imports, exports and coastal trade by all ships not flying the Chinese flag, regardless of whether the owners were foreigners or not. Officially, determining the customs tariffs was a joint task of the Chinese authorities and foreign managers, but in practice it was China's trading partners who set them. In 1901 the service's authority was extended to include the collection of all customs fees within a radius of 50 Chinese miles of the treaty ports. These fees, as well as the tax-free revenues of maritime customs, went exclusively to creditors as compensation payments for damages imposed upon the Chinese after the Boxer Rebellion.

It was not only the postal service that was subordinated to the powerful Maritime Customs Service. Foreign interests also ran the lighthouses along the coast and tugboat services in the treaty ports through the office. Not a single Chinese person was ever appointed to a position of responsibility at the IMCS during the first 50 years of its existence. When in July 1906 the Chinese government established its own finance office to control the customs service, the foreign powers saw their interests threatened. The Chinese side was trying to ensure over the longer run that, given the advanced age of Inspector-General Robert Hart, his successor could not be invested with such far-reaching powers. Their efforts paid off. During his years of service, the man who succeeded Hart, Sir Francis Aglen (1869–1932), never matched his predecessor's purview.

Until October 1911 the Maritime Customs Service took no direct part in collecting customs fees in the treaty ports, depositing them into bank accounts or transferring them to the various creditors. Through his local subordinates, the inspector-general was responsible simply for correctly setting the fees and informing the Chinese authorities of the revenues. Chinese and foreign traders paid their customs duties directly to Chinese banks selected and monitored by the IMCS. During the uncertain days of transition from imperial rule to republican governance in 1911–12, however, many Chinese officials fled the coastal cities for safer regions in the interior to escape personal injury in the disturbances. IMCS staffers feared that vacant positions would be filled by people who had no interest in continuing to service Chinese debt by using customs revenue for the foreigners' benefit. The port administrations then declared their independence from Beijing and continued to divert customs revenue – including previously accessible accounts – to foreign banks.

One of the first warnings to the young republican government over who exercised real authority in the country came when Beijing was compelled by the diplomatic corps to formally recognize these new structures. The agreement included the founding of a new international commission of bankers in Shanghai to monitor the Chinese government's prompt debt servicing and reparations payments. From then on the inspector-general was empowered to directly collect customs revenues in the ports, deposit these sums with so-called foreign custodian banks and transfer them 'to offset certain credits and compensation payments'. He was also responsible for forwarding the payments to creditors according to a priority guide that the commission of bankers determined. Implicitly, until 1921, China's foreign contractual partners had the authority to determine every year whether a surplus existed that could be transferred to the Chinese government.

The first time such a surplus was acknowledged was in 1917, when payments to some creditors, including Germany and Austria, had been discontinued because of the war. Also, the huge sums now being deposited at the custodian banks – namely HSBC (Hongkong & Shanghai Banking Corporation), the Deutsch-Asiatische Bank and the Russo-Asiatic Bank –

should have been made available to the Chinese government but were effectively lost to it, with the exception of the interest that was regularly transferred. The custodian banks could thus freely use these funds for their own commercial interests.[24]

FOURTEEN

The Japanese Invasion: *Trauma 9*

WHEN ONE CONSIDERS Japan's attitude towards China during these years, one is left with the impression that the Japanese were simply awaiting their chance to finally lead the international effort to enslave the Chinese people. The first step was the annexation of Korea in 1910, during the Qing Dynasty's terminal decline. On the island of Taiwan the Japanese acted brutally and mercilessly towards the non-Chinese indigenous population in many ways, but kept a certain degree of consideration toward the Chinese there. Those wishing to make their careers in the Japanese bureaucracy, for example, were required only to stop using Chinese and speak Japanese, including in private. In Korea the Japanese proceeded with an unparalleled cruelty that Koreans still recall with bitterness today. In a bid to erase Korean culture, the use of the Korean language was completely banned, even within the family.

The First World War saw Japan move closer to its visions of mainland dominion. The Japanese rightly concluded that they had more to gain by entering the war on the British side. The German colony, hopelessly far away from the homeland and garrisoned by a few thousand troops, was untenable. The Japanese captured Kiautschou Bay in 1914, the first year of the war, and held the defenders as prisoners of war in various camps until the war's end. One year later, the Japanese Empire issued its Twenty-one Demands to Yuan Shikai, the president of the Republic of China. These demands exceeded anything the Europeans had ever expected of China and marked the beginning of decades of Japanese annexation efforts, a large-scale invasion, the most appalling and inhuman war crimes against the Chinese people – later as Germany's ally in the Second World War – and finally the defeat of the Japanese Empire through the use of U.S.

atomic bombs, approved by President Harry Truman during the four-power Potsdam Conference on the future of Germany.

The Twenty-one Demands laid down Japan's claims to Shandong Province, Manchuria and Inner Mongolia, as well as China's southern coast and the mouth of the Yangtse River, as a preliminary step to achieving complete supremacy in China. Japan's logistical advantages as a country just off the Chinese coast already worked in its favour in the rivalry for dominance in China between the Europeans and the U.S. The Chinese would also be required to buy half their armaments from Japan in the future. Yuan Shikai had no choice but to bow to the Japanese ultimatum. After the war's end the Treaty of Versailles transferred Germany's lease on Kiautschou to the Empire of Japan. Chinese nationalists resented the U.S. for having declared Japan's claims in China legitimate in 1917 instead of advocating the German colony's return to China. Japan also received a League of Nations mandate over Germany's possessions in the Pacific north of the Equator. Only in 1922 did Japan desist from the Twenty-one Demands and return some of territorial gains in Shandong and the oil-rich northern half of Sakhalin Island back to the Chinese.

We need not recount further the details of Japan's subsequent encroachments on China from then until the end of the Second World War, when the Japanese withdrew from all the territories they claimed in China, including Taiwan and Korea. Even during the early years of the Chinese Republic, the traumas suffered by the once great empire led to profound changes that were both disrupted and stimulated by the Japanese invasion and military campaigns of the 1930s and '40s.

Looking back at the epochs covered by this summary of China's humiliations, one must conclude that none of the countries involved can claim only to have been a victim. However, as a consequence of public awareness of the great numbers of people killed or mutilated in the U.S. atomic bombings of Hiroshima and Nagasaki, the Japanese have managed to be remembered every year almost exclusively as victims of the Second World War, while hardly anyone remembers the countless human lives that Japan's war machine either extinguished or scarred physically or emotionally in mainland China and Southeast Asia. The victims of Japanese doctors' and soldiers' inhuman experiments on Chinese people during the Japanese occupation of Manchuria and those killed in the Nanjing Massacre are commemorated, at best, in China alone. In the rest of the world, except among small groups of scholars who deal professionally with these events, they have vanished from popular memory.[25]

The interventions of European countries cost far fewer lives, but their violations of Chinese sovereignty traumatized the overwhelming majority of China's people. The enormous economic damage that ruined China was not the country's only wound. The violation of conventional ideas of order within families, the state and the whole world and its hierarchies did profound damage among both the learned and the simple people of the cities and the countryside.

Of course, although it has been portrayed here as the victim of European, American and finally Japanese aggression from the early nineteenth century onward, China is itself no blank slate on the subject of expansion, annexation and aggression against its own neighbours. Had the Vietnamese not resisted the repeated efforts of the Chinese Empire to annex their country, China would today claim them as an integral part of the country, just as it does Tibet in the southwest and the once purely Uighur-populated regions in the west. China has taken advantage of weaker neighbours over the centuries, just as the Western powers have. If any lesson can be drawn from the apparently permanent ebb and flow of power in the world, it is that we have no reason to assume that borders between states will be safer in the future than they were in the past.

For the historian, this brief account does not primarily raise the question of how the once-mighty realm of Emperor Qianlong could, in the space of only two centuries, collapse in the dust and ash of revolution. Many answers, perhaps more than enough, have already been provided for that question. What seems more important today is the search for reasons why, 100 years after Chinese civilization appeared to have reached its nadir and apprehensive Chinese intellectuals saw the approaching demise of their national history in a social Darwinist extinction of the weak, China is back on top. Today it holds the world's largest foreign exchange reserves and its president travels self-confidently to the United States, where he is greeted by that country's head of state and treated to pomp and ceremony signifying a meeting of two equals. It is a process surely unmatched in history, of a civilization seemingly wrecked by another – and the Japanese were capable of mounting their aggression only because they had themselves become part of this other, Western civilization in its technological and scientific aspects – and then reviving within a relatively short time, and it demands explanations that historiography so far has not adequately provided.

PART III

A Clash of Cultures?

FIFTEEN

How Would You Have Reacted?

WITHOUT A DOUBT, the blow that caused the empire of China to stagger and eventually fall consisted in part of the unprecedented financial burdens that the Unequal Treaties forced the country to accept. More important – much more important – was the psychological trauma of being displaced from the centre of the civilized world and reduced to being a pawn of foreign powers. That included the unprecedented experience of neither mastering nor even comprehending the rules by which the imperialist powers acted. This trauma penetrated deep into the Chinese people's conception of themselves. It remains unhealed today and will probably continue to hurt indefinitely, both in the population's collective memory and in influencing both the domestic and foreign policies of the Chinese government. Today, errors of judgement committed again and again by European and American commentators become understandable when we recognize that they have not adequately considered this trauma's aftereffects.

'How would you have reacted?' one might ask the reader after recapitulating what was done to China in the nineteenth and early twentieth centuries. If China had collectively adopted the hatred that more than a few in the population felt and expressed in many ways towards the missionaries, the henchmen of the Western 'imperialists', and towards Western lifestyle and religion, science and technology, who would not sympathize?

Hatred does not only stem from injuries to one's basic values and traditional structures and hierarchies. It can also come from a sense of helplessness and inferiority toward the aggressor. It was no different in China, but – and this is the point of departure for the process that would rebuild China – hatred remained an understandable pattern of response that was limited to the individual. It did not ultimately guide China's response to the West's interventions.

China did not remain in the stupor of a profoundly humiliated individual who either gives up hope or thirsts only for revenge: revenge against a stronger adversary who has upended one's own values, which might be achieved through terrorism. Even in this situation of extreme subjective humiliation and insecurity, China demonstrated that it can come up with sensible and effective countermeasures to even the greatest challenges.

Make no mistake – a deep dislike certainly exists in China, a dislike that, in its most extreme manifestations, could be called hatred of those who have dishonoured China. Reliable studies that document the scale of this aversion are unknown, but many observers of China have the impression that, collectively, it is directed first and foremost at the Japanese, not the West. Still, this dislike is expressed principally in personal conversations and becomes public only when a concrete occasion for emotional reactions arises. The Chinese government gladly tolerates these reactions for a certain time, as these retroactively legitimize the CP's heroic role in the struggle against the Japanese invaders. In daily life and quotidian politics, however, this dislike can hardly be felt at all. Japanese products fill Chinese shelves. The producer country's proximity helps people believe that the cheapest way to get everything China needs to keep booming is to buy from Japan.

That may seem astonishing, given the horrific suffering that the Japanese caused in China in the 1930s and '40s. For the Japanese war criminals in Manchuria, the Chinese they tortured, on whom they conducted ghastly medical experiments and finally killed, were just *murata*, or 'logs'. After all, one can do what one likes with logs, including making firewood out of them when needed.[26] Does China keep reminding the world of these atrocities? It certainly does not. Memories of them remain chiefly internalized. Take Nanjing, for example. The memorial dedicated to the Siemens employee John Rabe is financed by Germany. In 1937 Rabe rescued thousands of Chinese people from certain death as the Japanese indiscriminately dragged hundreds of thousands of residents out of their apartments, and raped and murdered them in an unfathomable orgy of violence.[27] China remembers this time but does not include the entire world in its memorializing, and only very rarely calls on the perpetrator nation to face up to its responsibility. Very few youngsters in Japan are aware of the crimes that their politicians and soldiers once committed in China, and China does not insist that this should be otherwise.[28]

As we have seen, the interventions by the Western powers had a different character. Still, reaching deep into China's political, economic and territorial sovereignty, not to mention the collective psyche, they were sufficiently lasting to justify being called a perpetrator-victim relationship. The Westerners behaved in China as barbarians, as destroyers, as thieves, looters and oppressors. Their conduct made a mockery of the 'Christian values' they claimed to follow. China had every reason to respond to the debasement of its civilization with collective hatred. None of this is changed by the historical fact that many nations, such as Vietnam in the more distant past or numerous Tibetans more recently and especially during the so-called Cultural Revolution, likewise regarded China as a destroyer, oppressor and looter. Weighing who did which injustice to whom is an idle pursuit that only on some day of final judgement might result in a verdict. In real politics, as many examples have demonstrated, it is useless. For Chinese sensibilities, the decisive trauma was the fall from the sublime dominance of the Emperor Qianlong over distant peoples such as George III, to the Empress Regent Cixi's ignominious escape from these very people deep into the provinces.

In numerous accounts of modern Chinese history and the activities of Western nations sketched here, one reads about a movement to 'strengthen oneself', of the reforms and modernizations that finally elevated China back onto an even footing with the West and perhaps further. We read this as if, in the depths of humiliation, adopting a rival culture so as to regain one's status as the Middle Kingdom was the obvious response. That is precisely what it was not.

Today we see the alternatives at flashpoints along the fault-line between Western culture and non-Western civilization. These civilizations see many, if not all, of their traditional values as being threatened by modern Western lifestyles and have so far been unable to contribute to the technological, scientific and therefore economic progress that drives the modern world forward. We see that this perceived humiliation has spawned not only individual but also widespread collective hatred that finds its expression in terrorism. After surveying centuries of past greatness and globally unmatched cultural achievements, perhaps what is lacking is the self-assurance to accept the new from the outside and integrate one's own surviving patrimony with the external influences that are both necessary and useful.[29] The widespread hatred of the u.s. and of the Western lifestyle in general that the writings of the Egyptian intellectual Sayyid Qutb have sparked even in educated circles in the Islamic world since the 1950s is inconceivable in this collective form in China.[30]

China had this self-assurance and proved it to the whole world. That a great civilization seemingly defeated by another could recover so swiftly and again stand up to its ostensible conqueror was hardly to be expected and may even be histori-cally unparalleled. This was no normal reform and cannot be adequately grasped by being called a revolution, although a literal revolution made the recovery possible.

SIXTEEN

The Tradition of Existential Autonomy

TO EXPLAIN THIS unique phenomenon, we must first look very far back into Chinese history. It is not enough to say that Chinese reformers and revolutionaries saw a new world abroad and then made it work in China. Had they not encountered a receptive population among those tasked with carrying out the reforms and revolutions, those reformers and revolutionaries would never have succeeded. The key to understanding therefore lies in those aspects of Chinese culture that had long ago put down roots and then, in the immensely challenging encounter with Western civilization that had begun so disastrously, were again put to the test.

Studying the enduring aspects of Chinese culture that help explain the country's behaviour during the nineteenth and twentieth centuries takes us back to the beginnings of the Chinese Empire, to the Han Dynasty 2,000 years ago. At that time or perhaps even earlier, during the late Zhou period, the foundations were laid for an opposite point of view to the belief that had dominated since prehistoric times, namely that the living are largely externally controlled in their existence. This becomes clear in the Chinese view of sickness and health, since China responded to the collective trauma it suffered in modern times the same way its people do to individual illness.

Confucianism, Daoism and Legalism are the three social doctrines of ancient China most widely known beyond East Asia. They were conceived during a time when many states battled each other for supremacy. The 'Warring States Period' lasted from the fifth century to 221 BCE, when the first Emperor of the Qin defeated his last rivals and established the united Empire of China. During the Warring States Period, people lived believing that they were completely controlled by the deeds and misdeeds of their ancestors. Nine generations of the deceased were always being called to account for the crimes committed during their lives on earth. Each charge, and the punishment likely to follow, affected the well-being of the living. The living didn't stand a chance.

Given the mountain of misdeeds that nine generations of the dead had accumulated, it was no wonder that there was so much suffering on earth. Moreover, the world was populated by demons and spirits who had lost their lives on earth through some kind of injustice and had no purpose but to make mischief. There were practically no remedies for the suffering caused by the misconduct of one's ancestors. One could only struggle against the constant threat of demons by making alliances with the greatest powers, such as the sun, moon and stars, or enlisting the help of spells, exorcisms, fearsome pictures or characters or pungent substances. These strategies of exorcism were diverse and can hardly all be included in one book.[31]

It was a world of people who mistrusted the living, their own ancestors and demons. The world consisted of struggles for survival, and not only on the battlefield in one of the many conflicts between rival states. The atmosphere was poisoned even in the private lives of families. Only in this kind of soil could the idea of ancestral crimes that so afflicted the living flourish.

Confucianism, Daoism and Legalism are generally interpreted as three separate outcomes of efforts to end the centuries-old phase of each against all and return to law and harmony. That may well be, but even with all their discrepancies, these three social teachings share something that has yet to be recognized by historiography: they all seek the individual's existential self-determination. Confucianism, Daoism and Legalism pointed the way out of the world of mistrust. The philosopher Mengzi explained the necessity of trust for a healthy society:

When those who occupy lower positions are not protected by those higher up, the people will not allow themselves to be governed. To be protected by those higher up there is a WAY: only those who enjoy the trust of their friends will also be protected by the higher-ups. To enjoy the trust of one's friends, there is also a WAY: only those who serve and make their parents happy will reap the trust of their friends. To serve and make one's parents happy, there is also a WAY: only those who are honest with themselves can serve their parents in a way that will make them happy. To be honest with oneself, there is also a WAY: only those aware of what constitutes goodness can be honest with themselves. The truth is that honesty is the WAY of heaven; thinking about honesty is the WAY of humanity. This is how it has always been: only those who are honest can move others to action. Those who are not honest will never be able to move others.[32]

That is only one view of the importance of trust in society, but it is an oft-cited one. It captures quite faithfully the levels of intensity in relationships within a society that Mengzi imagined to be the alternative to the highly unsatisfactory situation of his time. The ruler's duty is to protect his subjects. Trust can exist only among friends. Children must be their parents' joy. All should be honest with themselves.

We can also let Confucius have his say on the subject: 'If the gentleman always acts respectfully and never does anything wrong, then all within the four seas will be his brothers. The gentleman will then never suffer from a lack of brothers.'[33] This dictum is constantly quoted in an abridged form and is therefore misleading. Confucius, such readings claim, said: 'Within the four seas [meaning in the whole world] all men are brothers.' That is precisely what he did not say. Only those who act like gentlemen will be associated so closely with other noble ones that they will be like brothers. Reality was and still is different.

Superficially, and helped by the efforts of individuals, these philosophers' appeals may have had some success, but within society at large they never achieved their goal. Chinese culture has always remained one of reciprocal suspicion, even among those closest to one another.

European parents and grandparents tell children fairy tales in which, after enduring all kinds of danger and evil, good people or goodness itself wins out in the end. This helps to instil a fundamentally positive, optimistic and trusting attitude towards life. In China, however, parents, grandparents and literature still tell stories from the time of the Warring States. Every Chinese person with even a cursory education is familiar, at least in its outlines, with the story of the war between the kingdoms of Yue and Wu in the fourth century BCE:

When young King Goujian ascended to the throne of Yue, King Helü of Wu considered this a good opportunity to attack Yue. He was defeated and mortally wounded, but before he died he managed to warn his son Fu Chai to 'never forget Yue!' Only three years later, Fu Chai defeated Yue and took King Goujian prisoner. Goujian worked for Fu Chai as a humble servant and thought constantly about how he might change matters to his advantage again. One day he heard that the king was suffering from diarrhea. He asked the king be informed that he wanted to eat his faeces. The taste would tell him, Goujian said, whether the illness was fatal. The king assented. Goujian tasted the faeces and said to the king that the illness would heal after a fairly long time. The king was so moved by the fact that Goujian had demeaned himself to eat his faeces only to be able to tell him that his illness would not be fatal that he set Goujian free. Having returned to his homeland, Goujian decided to sleep on a bed of firewood and hung over his head a bladder of animal bile, whose bitterness he tasted daily. In daily life he allowed himself none of the comforts, let alone luxuries, that are worthy of a king.

He resolved to change his circumstances only once he had taken his revenge. With his advisors he planned his next moves. He sent King Fu Chai the most beautiful woman in his kingdom, and indeed, Fu Chai fell in love and neglected governing more and more. He built a fantastic palace for his beloved. He wanted to place everything at her feet. When he told her, regretfully, that only the moon he could not bring down for her from the heavens, she answered that yes he could. He would only have to build a pond on a mountaintop, where the moon would be reflected and then scooped up. And that is what happened. Ten years passed before Yue dared to attack. In a first campaign Goujian killed the crown prince of Wu. In a second one he besieged the capital of Wu for three years and finally took it. When he stood before King Fu Chai, Fu Chai said to him, 'But I allowed you to live.' 'That was your mistake!' Goujian responded and killed him. Afterwards he also had all of Fu Chai's advisors killed, and finally his own.[34]

This story cannot be compared with the tricks used by the Valiant Little Tailor to impress the king, overcome the giant and finally marry the princess, nor is it comparable with the saga of the wily Odysseus. Both these stories have happy endings and give rise to a positive atmosphere conducive to the hopefulness in which basic trust can grow. The Tailor's wedding brings the cleverest of all onto the throne, and the return of Odysseus reunites two people who belong together, namely the spouses whom the war had separated.

The Chinese story teaches a completely different moral. Instead of the struggle of good against evil, the dynamic at work here is outright cunning and the gaining of advantage. The most devious character wins, but the reader can be sure that the next schemer will soon arrive to capitalize when opportunity knocks. It never stops. There is no happy ending. The attitude thus taught is one of always staying alert and of inventing stratagems.[35] It became the psychological legacy of the Warring States Period, propagating itself from century to century. It vies with pleas, repeated from ancient times to the present day, for 'harmony.'

To be sure, the harmony that especially the Confucians sought was a concession to the multitude of interests and cultural currents that collided during the Warring States Period and would finally coexist after the empire's foundation in one civilization. Forcing all these currents into one riverbed seemed impossible. Therefore the sought-after harmony was not one of unison, but of many voices that nonetheless produced beautiful music. The principle was the same as that of a meal consisting of not just one kind of meat or vegetable but an assortment of foods, spices and other ingredients that together are pleasing to the palate. Harmony within a society that from the beginning was as heterogeneous and complex as that of China remained an exalted goal that, though periodically invoked, has never been completely attained.

Of course, appeals of this sort are pointless if people are convinced that their lives are steered by a fate determined somewhere else – in heaven, in hell or by demons. These are precisely the facets of ancient thought that the new philosophies challenged. Viewed today, the point of transition from the old ideas of total existential dependence to the new teaching of existential self-determination is unclear. A student of Confucius, Zi Xia, is said to have told the master that, 'I have heard the following: death and life are destiny; heaven decides over nobility and wealth.'[36] The master did not comment on this statement. Unsurprisingly, one can still read inscriptions on Buddhist temples saying, 'What man plans cannot be compared to what heaven plans.' Was this an alliance between the Confucians and religion, which has always fundamentally denied people's existential free will and stressed that human destiny is inextricably bound to the unfathomable decisions of heaven, or of the one God in the West?

We do not know how Confucian the line from Zi Xia about the power of destiny is. The fact is that Confucianism prescribed to people a variety of behaviours called rituals that could be applied to every part of life and every personal relationship. Following these rituals was the key to social harmony and personal well-being. Confucianism taught – as a means of challenging a reality that suggested the opposite – a belief in the goodness that is either innate in people or can at least be instilled during upbringing. In no way must this upbringing be non-violent. A young person is like a piece of wood that has grown crooked and must be straightened and planed: splinters will inevitably fall, wrote the philosopher Xunzi in the third century BCE. Yet there was much more at stake.

At stake was the liberation, indeed the forcible expulsion, of people from the mindset of deceit and constant spying on one another and to remake them into good people. Customs, morals, rituals and education were the ways and means of giving people the possibility of determining their own lives and finding individual well-being and social harmony. Heaven, the new message said, may well rule over life and death, but through his own conduct, the individual can in many ways help ensure that life becomes more bearable and does not end prematurely. Confucius did not care to speculate over an afterlife. It would be best not to think about it at all, after which the superstition would die out, he probably thought.

For the Daoists, the many local deities that made life miserable for people were likewise suspect. The Daoists did not go as far as the Confucians, who turned a blind eye to the question of the existence and influence of demons and deities. Yet the Daoists also sought to break the cycle of dependency. They directed the attention of the living to the powers in heaven that might help them banish the powers of the underworld. Independence from the powers of the underworld was what turning to Dao promised, the Way that presents itself to humans through an anthropomorphic pantheon. The mayhem brought upon people by the forces of darkness can be undone only by the representatives of the Dao, the Daoist priests. One can keep one's health by living in accordance with the Dao, according to their teaching. A life lived this way denies the powers of darkness their sway over human existence.[37]

The same milieu also gave rise to the idea that one must adopt the way of nature, turn one's back on advanced culture and be satisfied with the simple things in life. In that way one avoids the temptations that drive people to compete over scarce resources and become deceitful and suspicious of one another. As we can read in chapter 80 of the *Daodejing*, rejection of complex culture was not limited to weapons, transportation systems and writing. The Daoists considered that the morality that the Confucians held up as a panacea for the morbid lack of harmony in the world was just another sign of evil. Morality as defined by people, they preached, is nothing but man-made coercion, leading – as all force does – to resistance and thereby to more of the endless suffering it is supposed to overcome.

That also places the Daoists in opposition to the Legalists, who received their name because they introduced laws – *leges* – to society as an effective means of constraining people, whom they believed were fundamentally evil, and forcing them to behave. To be sure, the term 'law' does not quite capture what the Legalists presented to the people as norms or measures. The Chinese word *fa* also includes meanings such as 'example' and 'pattern'.

The basic idea is the norm that each must adhere to in order to avoid punishment. All the social doctrines took *fa* into consideration. For the Confucians it denoted the exemplary lives of the ancient sages. For the Daoists it was the pattern or scheme of natural processes that had to be adjusted to, and for the Legalists it meant the laws before which all were equal, even including, as some demanded, the emperor!

In all of these interpretations, however, *fa* provided the basis for questioning the individual's fundamental helplessness against external determination. At some point during the later Zhou or early Han Dynasty, in the first or second century BCE, people came upon the idea that laws were more than the basis for an orderly society. The new insight found that laws were also the foundations for the eternal order of nature. If people could recognize these laws and keep them, they could be shielded from all manner of trouble and sickness and live their earthly lives to the full.

Just as in Greece a few centuries earlier, in ancient China the gates were thrown open to a philosophy that distanced itself from the fundamental control of external, numinous forces that had previously been considered all-powerful. Suddenly it all made sense: those who keep the laws of society remain free of punishment and live in peace to a ripe old age. Added to this realization was a second element: those who live by the laws of nature keep sickness at bay and live long, healthy lives. Was this new outlook Confucian, Daoist or Legalist, or perhaps an insight that spanned all of these social doctrines? What we do know is that perhaps the earliest outright statements based on this outlook can be found in the *Suwen*, a classic Han Dynasty text that at first glance deals with medicine, but actually, as has often been the case in Chinese history, spreads new and provocative philosophical and political opinions under the guise of medical theory and practice.

In the first or second century CE a compiler whose name we do not know collected hundreds of statements by equally unknown authors from the previous one or two centuries and assembled them into an artificial dialogue, mostly between the Yellow Thearch Huang Di and an expert named Hippo(crates?). Again and again, the compiler included statements in this dialogue that demonstrated that people could lead their own autonomous lives. It centred on two key ideas: *fa* or laws/norms/ examples, and *ming* or fate.

The Chinese word for fate, *ming* (命), is also found in the dictionary under 'order' and 'mandate'. Indeed, people live – according to the original idea – because they have the 'mandate' of heaven to exist. Heaven can withdraw this mandate at any time. That is death. People have no power over this mandate; it hangs from the strings of heaven. The *Suwen* gives a completely different reading: 'If one carefully follows the WAY (dao 道) as the laws (fa 法) [have ordered], then the mandate of heaven will last long.'[38]

This turned the existing view of things on its head. It is not the mandate of heaven that determines how long people live. By following the Way, people hold the power in their own hands to decide how long the mandate lasts. At another point this statement is repeated, this time somewhat laden with medicinal accessories:

When one carefully follows the way (dao 道) as the laws (fa 法) [ordain it], then one will achieve myriad healings in myriad cases. Qi and blood will reach the right balance and the heavenly mandate will last long.[39]

That is explicit enough. Again, the *fa* – the laws – are included. People must submit to the laws – whether of society or of nature remains unstated – after which people hold their 'mandate' – or fate – in their own hands. How do people obtain their lives? Not thanks to heaven or other numinous influences. Simply put, it is the secular processes of nature that enable the existence of human beings as the crown, not of nature, but of all earthly things.

> Vaulted by the heavens and buttressed by the earth, the 10,000 things come into existence. No one is nobler than man. Man receives his life from Qi from heaven and earth. He matures by the laws of the four seasons.[40]

The message that permeates this new medicine is that health – for most people the greatest concern of their earthly lives – does not hinge on the actions of gods, spirits, demons, ancestors or an abstract 'heaven'. Instead, it is up to each person to shape the length and quality of life by keeping to the *fa*.

This was the background against which a battle cry emerged that one day must have alarmed all those who did not want to grant the people any freedom in their lives. The battle cry was that 'I, and not heaven, am responsible for my fate!'[41] The earliest author associated with this slogan is Ge Hong, 'the master who embraces simplicity', *baopuzi*, in the fourth century. Later it is also found in the works of another Daoist named Tao Hongjing, around the year 500. Wherever it arises, it is the rallying cry of those determined to take their fate into their own hands when calling others to join them.

To be completely faithful in terms of grammar and content, we can also translate the exhortation of Ge Hong and Tao Hongjing thus: 'I confer the mandate upon myself, heaven does not confer it!' To make it clear that people have the means to extend the 'mandate' indefinitely on their own, Ge Hong added a reference to alchemy, the 'science' of the Daoists that would translate existential self-determination into reality. With the help of the elixir, Ge Hong believed, one can extend one's life indefinitely. The supposed mandate of heaven is meaningless, the alchemist wrote.

That was also the time during which the building blocks were put in place for a Chinese explanation of the world that approached the mysteries of things completely differently from the foundations that had only recently been laid in Europe of what would later become the natural sciences. Two secular, non-religious approaches to an understanding of what holds the world together existed in Greece and China. We can call the first approach analytical and the second relationist. In Europe the analytical approach prevailed. Always in search of the *atomos*, it held that one had to find the smallest elemental building blocks of things to then understand the entirety (*compositum*) of these building blocks in its essence.

Though they did not fall completely silent in Europe, the voices who refused to accept this approach as the right way to understand the nature of things dwindled to only a few philosophers. It was Auguste Comte who pointed out in the mid-nineteenth century, before analytical science began its triumphal march through the world, that

> man can grasp neither the nature nor the origin and certainly not the purpose of the phenomena that surround him. One can only meaningfully concern oneself with the relationships among phenomena. If these are not random but lasting and constant, they can, however, permit the construction of terms regarding their similarities and of laws regarding their sequences.[42]

Even if these thoughts came from the first protagonist of European Positivism, they are also suited to a brief sketch of the relationist approach toward nature that became prevalent in China. Comte did not believe that breaking things down in the manner of analytic research was a helpful way to understand them. To arrive at something's nature, the point was rather to study the ways in which it interacts and combines with other things.

By the 1970s, when China was opening up and acupuncture was coming to epitomize Chinese medicine, the concepts of Yin and Yang had entered the global vocabulary. Together with a second, secular model for explaining all existence called the Five Phases, the Yin-Yang doctrine emerged during the second half of the first millennium BCE, during the so-called Warring States Period. The two carry the psychological legacy of that period into the present day. The Yin-Yang doctrine is nothing but a recognition of the normality of violence. The day destroys the night; the night takes revenge and destroys the day. This principle suffuses all nature. It governs the succession of dynasties just as it does all interaction among people. By acknowledging the everyday nature of violence, the Yin-Yang and Five Phases doctrines also teach how to survive in this violent environment. Yin-Yang and the Five Phases are not meant to break things down to their constituent elements to explain their emergence, existence and passing. They focus solely on the relationships among all phenomena, arranging these into groups based on behaviour and showing how these groups interact.

For two millennia the analytical approach of European culture tried to explain and manipulate all natural phenomena. The relationist approach in Chinese culture was also applied for 2,000 years to interpret all existence. Only in the eighteenth, nineteenth and especially the twentieth century did these two systems become direct rivals. In nearly all challenges in everyday life, the analytical approach proved superior to the relationist.

Both approaches strive for the goal of any of the natural sciences: that is, to arrive at natural laws that apply independently of space, time and earthly and numinous powers. They serve to give people guidelines that will set the courses for their lives. That leaves no room for the impenetrable decree of God or the whims of spirits, deities, ancestors or demons. The slogan 'I, and not heaven, am responsible for my fate' expressed the quintessence of the new thinking.

Therefore the new medicine that emerged in the centuries preceding and during the first millennium CE focused on demonstrating to people the possibilities for leading their lives autonomously. *Ming*, meaning 'mandate' or 'fate', was not the only term that was reinterpreted. Even more important was the revolution of power between people and spirits. In the new medicine, man holds the spirits captive in his organs. It therefore depends on each individual whether the spirits stay contained or attain freedom – in which case they can do mischief and cause harm to people.

Consequently, there were two sides to this coin, of course. Liberating oneself from the interference of inscrutable forces meant that each individual must shoulder responsibility for his or her own welfare. Confucianism and Legalism proved to be particularly unfeeling, emotionless and schematic instructions. Those who failed to keep the laws and the examples of the sages, those who disregarded rituals and behavioural norms had only themselves to blame if they were punished or forfeited their lives. There was little mercy here, and even less charity. Only Buddhism would bring a measure of warmth to China through Guanyin, the goddess who, with a thousand eyes, seeks out those who suffer and, with a thousand hands, helps those who cannot help themselves.

The seminal text of Chinese medicine, the *Suwen*, repeats, staccato-like: 'Above and below, the same rules apply everywhere!'[43] Chinese medicine itself postulates an extreme form of individualism that does not fit at all with our image of Chinese culture. The central doctrine of causes holds that every illness stems from an inability to control one's emotions. Wherever emotions are not curbed, they damage the organs with which they are linked: excessive joy harms the heart, excessive planning hurts the liver and so on. Only once this kind of damage exists can external pathogenic factors penetrate the human organism and cause illness in the body. According to this view, everyone is responsible for their own happiness – as well as their own misery.

While now briefly shifting our attention to Europe, we must keep this facet of Chinese culture – the individual responsibility for happiness and sorrow, health and illness – in the backs of our minds together with the still-predominant principle of mistrust. For we are seeking the longstanding facets of Chinese culture that will help us explain how China managed to rise

from the great trauma caused the Western and Japanese imperialist powers in the space of a few decades.

'How would you have reacted?', we asked earlier. Answering
this question is not easy. But in European civilization, some
forces have been at work for centuries that did not exist in Chinese culture. Perhaps these differences are important in understanding China's actual response to the humiliations it endured.

SEVENTEEN

Europe and the Discovery of Social Welfare

UNTIL THE LATE eighteenth century the development of Europe in some ways resembled that of China. The secular, non-religious, analytical explanation of the world gradually evolved into natural science. Christian theologians always watched this tendency with suspicion and occasionally even considered the murder of this or that scientist to be justified if it helped preserve the influence of theology. Yet over the centuries European science accumulated more and more insights that helped liberate people from what theologians saw as the unknowable will of God or, in the scientists' view, the rigours of nature. The growing appreciation of the laws of nature served to unshackle people from all the restrictions that nature had imposed upon them.

The aeroplane overcame humans' inability to fly. Highly complex prosthetic devices eased the disabilities of amputees. To relax the strictures facing the human mind, computers were introduced to work alongside it as electronic brains. Theologians protested vigorously whenever another threshold seemed to have been crossed on the way towards perfecting the human organism, freeing it from pain and fulfilling most people's wishes for lasting good health. Yet Europe's analytical science also set in motion a process of existential self-determination that remained closed to China's relationist science.

As European science conveyed the message that behaving according to the dictates of the laws of nature helps people to avoid sickness, it also placed responsibility for illness itself on the individual. In the course of almost two millennia, this individualized responsibility obviated the need for any healthcare policy worthy of the name today. Minimal steps were enacted here and there to remedy the most deplorable conditions, but there was no conceptual basis for the comprehensive, caring intervention of a government authority.

That changed in Europe – indeed, only in Europe – during the later eighteenth century. The transformation was admirably captured in two influential books that were published in quick succession and could not have been more different. The first of these, *The Divine Order in the Circumstances of the Human Sex, Birth, Death and Reproduction*, was written by a theologian named Johann Peter Süssmilch (1707–1767). Süssmilch was the first – *cum grano salis* – medical statistician. The long tables of figures he compiled convinced him that God's plan was behind the regularities of birth, sickness and death. They still remind us today that statistics can be used to back up any opinion one might wish to advance. Completing the irony, Germany's medical statisticians named their professional association after Süssmilch.

Soon after this theological statistician 'proved' that human destiny was controlled by unknowable forces, a physician influenced by Rousseau named Johann Peter Frank (1745–1821) reached some very different conclusions. Most human illnesses, Frank demonstrated in his multi-volume work,[44] are influenced by human behaviour and can therefore be avoided by acting accordingly.

At first glance, his seemed like just another voice in the unending struggle between those who deny human autonomy and those who, ever since Socrates, have championed it. Yet it was the product of something completely new. Frank did *not* follow the pattern of doctors since ancient times of advising patients to maintain their health by keeping the six *res non-naturales* and *res contra naturam*.[45] Instead he called on the state to begin helping people to maintain good health at the point where their own responsibility ends. His means of accomplishing this was a 'medical police' or, in today's parlance, a public healthcare policy. His lecture 'On Social Misery as the Mother of Illness', which he gave in Pavia in 1790, pointed the direction that such a policy should take.

This was new. People can do much to protect themselves from becoming ill – eating right, getting enough (but not too much) sleep, working and resting enough, and so on. But Frank apparently opened people's eyes to the conditions under which others were living – conditions they had little power to change. Working conditions, living conditions, environmental conditions and other circumstances were suddenly brought to the attention of those with power. Until then, worldly and ecclesiastical rulers had hardly ever had to seriously concern themselves with the health of their subjects. Structures and priorities, however, were changing.

The gradual replacement of feudal government with nation-states was what actually caused politicians to begin paying attention to this new concern. New forms of interstate rivalry accompanied the emergence of nation-states. The wars of the French Revolution vividly demonstrated the superiority of armies motivated by patriotism over existing mercenary forces. The workshops that would soon grow into major industries needed strong, healthy males of all social classes who could cope with long, hard workdays. Such strong, healthy men – and the strong, healthy women who gave birth to them – became the most important pillars of the state during both war and peace. It was not some humanitarian virus that had infected those in power, but the economic theories of mercantilism that focused attention on 'conditions.'

The 'conditions' had always been there, and the medical profession had always kept an eye on them. In the Hippocratic writings, authors we no longer know by name instruct others to ask about a patient's line of work. For governments and official authorities, of course, this medical knowledge played no role at all for nearly 2,000 years. In more recent times the physicians Paracelsus (1493–1541) and Agricola (1494–1555) devoted attention to the grossly unhealthy lives that miners lived, which frequently ended prematurely through arsenic, lead and/or mercury poisoning. In his work *De morbis artificum diatriba,* Bernardino Ramazzini (1633–1714) counted 40 work-related sicknesses and drew attention to the 'conditions' that caused them. Yet the impulses that drive politics are always cynical. Only once the economic and military advantages of doing so had become clear did authorities pay attention to the individual suffering of people and enact countermeasures.

This was the advent of a defining European cultural trait and one of that civilization's greatest achievements: the inclusion of social welfare in politics. The effects were various and in no way limited to the health of the population. The social element of European policymaking soon embraced another characteristic of ancient Europe: democracy. The amalgamation of these two elements into social democracy further enhanced European power, lifting it above all other civilizations. The new attention to conditions, whether in society or in the natural environment, necessarily shifted responsibility, both for what people suffered and what they could themselves do to change these conditions.

The first to come under scrutiny were the miners, then 40 other professions, and finally the special conditions under which women, children, populations of certain regions, ethnic groups and the workforce in general had to endure. The consequence was collective political thought and action. Not every worker was doing badly; not every woman was suffering. Yet altogether, these groups as a whole were still affected. But how could a collective take action? Political leaders might emerge from its midst, or outside advocates might offer their services for the common good and change the conditions. But how could these changes begin? At least two possibilities could be considered. First, there was acting under one's own volition. The principle here, if 'we' were doing badly, would be for us to change the conditions of our existence to make them more bearable. The alternative would be to transfer responsibility to those we believe are to blame. 'We are doing badly because of you, so you have to improve the conditions of our existence.'

Europe has seen both approaches, yet its politics are increasingly marked by the simpler approach: of transferring responsibility for changing the unsatisfactory conditions – that is, the disadvantages – that some people face, to those identified as their actual or supposed cause. This mentality neglects indi-

vidual initiative and responsibility. One might claim to see a de-
marcation line between conservative and leftist forces here, but
these political approaches do not quite line up with the contours
of political parties. The social-democratic element of European
civilization has become deeply anchored in all parties, even
those that do not carry these catchwords in their names. The
spectrum of political parties may vary significantly in the levels
of individual initiative and responsibility that are expected from
affected groups in changing their conditions. Yet the general
principle remains essentially unaffected. Today all the parties
of Europe are 'leftist'.

To recapitulate, both in Europe and in China, trust in the
ubiquity and autonomy of the laws of nature was the condition
for people's pursuit of existential self-determination. In medicine as in social behaviour, however, responsibility for how good
and long one's life was remained for 2,000 years with the
individual. By the early eighteenth century, the attitude that the
individual was part of both society and nature began to take
hold. Society and the natural environment impose conditions
that do not fall under the responsibility of the individual and
yet substantially influence his or her welfare. To match the new
outlook in Europe, the liberating Chinese slogan 'I, and not
heaven, am responsible for my fate' would have to be reworded
as 'Conditions are responsible for our fate and we can change
them'. Each individual's responsibility for his or her own life is
augmented by the demand for society to take political action
where conditions that burden people's lives are beyond the
responsibility of those they affect.

For much of the population of Europe, the process has parted
company with the original, sensible balance between individual
and external responsibility for people's lives. The predominant
mentality is now a different one: 'We are not responsible for our
fate. Conditions are, and changing them is the responsibility of
those who cause them.' This attitude has remained a European
one. It has never taken root in China, despite Marxism-Leninism
and the so-called Communist Party. We will return to this when
we examine the role of Marxism in China as the ideology that

played the guiding role in restoring the country's sovereignty and dignity against Japanese and Western greed as well as in reordering the structure of Chinese society.

EIGHTEEN

China Takes Its Fate into Its Own Hands

LET US AT this point recall a truism that, since we have been referring to 'China' so frequently as a collective, must nonetheless be repeated again and again: just like every country and every culture, China is in no sense a homogeneous entity. Since ancient times, China has always produced a variety of opinions, philoophies and, in times of crisis, proposed solutions. And yet, China is indeed a collective. Its people see themselves as such, frequently act as such and, indeed, must be regarded as such. Innumerable Chinese individuals made their fortunes by helping to enslave young Chinese men and sell them to Portuguese traders. Countless Chinese individuals also became rich by joining the opium trade and poisoning their own nation. All of these individuals are part of the Chinese collective, but this collective's overall behaviour has not necessarily served the purposes of particular interests.

The collective's behaviour has followed reaction patterns that transcend particular interests and are deeply rooted in Chinese culture. China is led by a party that calls itself 'Communist', and Marxism-Leninism is still broadly present in the country's academic institutions. Still, the mentality which stems from a sense of helplessness and surrender, of transferring responsibility for unsatisfactory conditions to those who supposedly caused them or to some 'responsible other', has remained largely alien to China, both collectively and for individuals – and herein lies the key to understanding the country's spectacular recovery.

Ideas that inform collective political action matured at some point in the mind of an individual. When, afterwards, many people choose, embrace and follow them from the great selection of ideas available at all times, these ideas must have fulfilled at least two conditions. They must meet certain basic values shared by these people and support solutions upholding those values, therefore appearing sensible. Over the long run the actions of a government, irrespective of its political system, generally reflect those shared values.

Up to the present day, China has remained a culture that integrates many different views of the world. Religious groups are just as much a part of this diversity as are those individuals who refuse to submit to the Communist Party's officially sanctioned view of society and world events. On the Internet these dissenters can, at least for short periods of time, share their opinions with other Internet users before official censors delete their remarks. And yet, despite this irrefutable heterogeneity, one can just as irrefutably identify the overarching collective consensus of the great majority, if not practically the entire population, in the Chinese response to the country's humiliation.

By the late nineteenth century, numerous Chinese observers had come to recognize the harsh reality that many aspects of their culture and science were inadequate as a means of curbing the inroads of Western nations into their land. Many of these voices began calling for profound and wide-ranging reforms. Other Chinese people vehemently opposed these demands. The advocates of reform prevailed and China went down the path of renewal.[46]

It was initially a feeble effort, with some reformers attempting to adopt only those aspects of Western technology, especially military technology, that were indispensible for defeating the invaders with their own weapons. Other more astute observers quickly recognized that this would not suffice. Gradually the need for a merciless self-analysis was acknowledged, along with the recognition that China would not only have to open itself superficially to the invaders' culture, but radically, in the true sense of the word. The transformation would have to reach all the way down to the roots of Chinese values and traditions.

China did not go down the path of hating the West for violently and contemptuously destroying the unmatched continuity of Chinese civilization. The Chinese did not simply hand responsibility for the wrongs they had suffered to the perpetrators and go cap in hand asking for alms and compensation. Following the old maxim of Ge Hong and Tao Hongjing, 'I, and not heaven, am responsible for my fate', China turned its gaze onto itself, sought culpability in its own insufficiencies and resolved to make changes from within that would put the country in a position to deal with the agents of its humiliation on its own terms. This was in no way a simple reform or modernization as depicted in many works on modern Chinese history. It was a 100-year cultural revolution with the objectives of uncovering all weaknesses and making good the obvious deficiencies by adopting the characteristics and achievements of European culture.

For China as a whole and, more importantly, for countless individuals, the so-called Great Proletarian Cultural Revolution of the 1960s and '70s, which was hostile to both Western influence and the country's own traditions, was a brutal caesura in this path.

Tracing the path toward this interruption need not concern our account of China's response to its humiliation at the hands of the West. The fact, however, that this break was overcome after only ten years, autonomously and without foreign help, despite the bitterest opposition and a gravely weakened economy, demonstrates clearly enough that the collective was willing and able to take a completely different course – and to see it through.

NINETEEN

First Steps to a New Beginning

WHEN THE WESTERN powers set about slicing up, dividing and perhaps digesting the Chinese cake, they confronted a great civilization that commanded the sincere respect of more than a few European observers. Long neglected in Western history books, China's contributions to global culture, science and technology had by then been portrayed in several striking accounts for a Western readership unable to read the Chinese sources itself.[47]

Countless findings that we would ascribe today to chemistry, physics, mathematics, astronomy, botany and biology are found in the (similarly innumerable) writings of Chinese scholars and nature-watchers of the past 2,000 years. Technological wonders of all kinds still elicit the highest admiration for the many historical figures whose precise observations and incisive conclusions provided solutions to many problems, whether in the exploitation of mineral resources, such as early underground drilling for salt, processing raw materials, facilitating transportation or other challenges of everyday life.

The backdrop to many of these achievements was the Confucian ideals, such as the eight goals formulated in the Book of Rites (*Liji*), possibly even before the founding of the empire in 221 BCE: investigating things, advancing knowledge, being of sincere mind, correcting consciousness, caring for the body, regulating family affairs, keeping order and establishing peace on earth.[48] The first two goals, of investigating things and moving knowledge forward, were declared essential not least by the Song-era philosopher Zhu Xi (1130–1200). Maxims like this need to be specified further, and for this, too, we find ample illustrations among later authors who seem quite familiar to us.

Chen Xianzhang (1428–1500), for example, stated:

The organizational principle inherent in things can be known only by personal experience through direct observation and then consideration. Personal experience is more valuable for the accumulation of knowledge then the wisdom of the ancient classics.[49]

Could there be a more explicit call – at the same time as similar statements in Europe – to leave the old behind and explore what is new? Does the modern reader not recognize the foundations of modern science being laid at the time in Europe reflected in the words of the same author, who wrote:

Be sceptical and then investigate further! Investigate further and so arrive at knowledge. Arrive at true knowledge and then find your beliefs, because doubt is the starting point of the path that leads to the Dao.

This kind of manifestos cannot essentially change collective attitudes toward traditional knowledge. There were simply no lacunae in the pre-modern Chinese perception of real things and their inherent nature that would have suggested turning away from the relationist view of nature and the veneration of ancient wisdom. Over the centuries, theories of systematic correspondence kept expanding into highly complex explanatory models, but they remained only that – explanatory models that were practically devoid of predictive capacity and which did nothing to help attain the knowledge and technological achievements with which so many clever people enriched Chinese civilization. The two remained two separate areas.

These theories did not provide China's enormous knowledge and astonishing technological skills with the appropriate accompanying logic to enable them to successfully stand up to Western science and technology. Once the direct confrontation with the analysis-based and future-facing European sciences and technologies culminated in China's bitter defeat, it did not at first seem that everything China had achieved in these areas needed to be discarded, however.

The first response of some attentive Chinese leaders to the imperial powers' obvious military and technological superiority was a logical one, given the country's historical experiences. Other countries had better weapons; these would first have to be acquired, then copied. Finally the foreigners would be defeated with their own weapons. Even Lin Zexu, the commissioner whose vigorous intervention in Canton led to the so-called First Opium War, ordered the purchase of several hundred European rifles and a European ship. That could not prevent his defeat, since no one really knew how to use the rifles. They were reserved for officers and served as status symbols instead of as tactical arms.[50]

In 1861 a new term appeared that expressed for the first time an admission of Chinese inferiority in the encounter with the Europeans: *ziqiang,* or 'strengthening oneself.' For about three decades, well into the 1890s, the illusion persisted that China's still superior civilization simply had to help itself to some of the barbarians' technical specialities in order to return to a normal state of affairs. German arms were especially popular in China for a while and raised hopes that this kind of 'strengthening oneself' could have the desired effect.[51] The German military victory against France in 1871 again raised Chinese hopes that by using the same weapons they, too, might defeat the French.[52]

Efforts at 'strengthening oneself' originated from a handful of members of the central government who soon made names for themselves as reformers, especially the Manchu Prince Gong (1833–1898) and another Manchu official, named Wenxiang (1815–1876). An initial reaction to the ominous shadow the foreigners were casting over China was the establishment, in 1861, of an 'Office for Executing Affairs with All Foreign States.' It became known by the name Zongli Yamen. Prince Gong swiftly rose to become the outstanding figure of this first Chinese foreign ministry's five-man board of directors. Wenxiang was war minister for a time and worked together with Prince Gong in the Zongli Yamen.

Only one year later, in 1862, Prince Gong and Wenxiang secured the establishment of China's first language school, which taught English and French. The age of the students – fourteen and under – clearly shows how long-term the plans actually were. Before long, five other language schools had been founded in Shanghai, Canton and Fuzhou. In 1867 Gong and Wenxiang recommended that the Beijing language school be turned into a modern college that would teach subjects such as mathematics, chemistry, geology, mechanics and international law. Conservatives resisted fiercely. They saw no need to learn from the barbarians, especially such marginal subjects.[53]

The conflicts that accompanied every step the reformers took have been detailed in the many books written about this transitional phase of Chinese history. Important milestones pushed through by the reformers included the founding of the first arms factories in Anqing and Jiangnan to study Western techniques of building cannon and ships in 1861 and 1865; of a new shipyard in Fuzhou in 1866; of the Naval Academy in Fujian in 1867; and of a teaching institute for telegraphy in Tianjin in 1879.[54]

Attention gradually turned from weapons to logistics. As sources of raw materials were prospected for a manufacturing industry, new transport and communications routes were needed, as was a completely new economic structure. Since the Chinese budget was at this time already heavily weighed down by war costs and reparations and the domestic situation had been weakened by rebellions, officials hoped to improve revenues that would in turn finance the mounting expenditures by reorganizing the economic system. Yet attention to the surrounding political and economic framework that had made Europe's expansion beyond its own borders possible in the first place remained non-existent.

Instead, it was hoped that a proven, 2,000-year-old strategy would make up for the country's military deficiencies: 'Keep the barbarians in check with barbarians.'[55] During the fifth century China succeeded in playing off against each other two enemy nations that threatened the country . During the Song dynasty, when the Jurchen people and the Liao were becoming dangerous to China, the government tried the same approach but the results were anything but those they had intended. Encouraged to fight the Liao, the Jurchen did just that – and with such success that they soon turned just as successfully against the Song. Now, in the late nineteenth century, the Chinese government tried once more to provoke the foreigners to fight each other, and failed again.

In 1863 the Chinese attempted to drive a wedge between the British and the French. Li Hongzhang (1823–1910), the intellectual leader of the self-strengthening movement, included Prussia in his political calculations as a potential trouble-maker within the European bloc. He later even took the trouble of travelling to Germany, where he met with Bismarck in 1896. After his return, Li Hongzhang was called 'the Bismarck of China'. Yet the possibilities of agitating the foreigners against each other remained very remote and the extension of this principle to the strategy of defeating the barbarians with their own weapons did not bring the success for which the Chinese had hoped. Japan's victory in the mid-1890s against a numerically superior Chinese army that was also seemingly ideally equipped with Krupp arms put an end to the illusions of 'strengthening oneself'.

Despite his understanding of the Europeans' technological superiority, Li Hongzhang – a loyal servant of his emperor – was still utterly convinced that China's intellectual culture was unsurpassed. He could not yet comprehend that the entirety of China's knowledge had to be put to the test.[56] Zhang Zhidong thought the same. In 1898 he published a book that was recommended by the imperial court and distributed by the million throughout the country. It attempted a tightrope walk between preserving a civilization grounded in the ancient Confucian classics of Chinese thinking on the one hand and studying useful Western ideas and skills on the other.[57] This is also the sense in which one should see the great translation project that rendered a total of 178 Western books into Chinese between 1871 and 1905. Sixty-six titles were in the natural sciences, 38 in military affairs, 35 in engineering, eleven in medicine, seven in agriculture and 21 in history.[58] Li Hongzhang and Zhang

Zhidong were hardly alone in their views, but given the country's bleak condition, calls for a truly profound renewal, for a 'young' or 'new' China that had to start again from the beginning, were growing stronger.[59]

The beginnings of serious study of the differences between Western and Chinese philosophy came from a man named Yan Fu (1854–1921), who was the first to bring sophisticated works of the European intellectual tradition to a Chinese readership, first only regionally in a daily newspaper in Tianjin and later through translations of Huxley's *Evolution and Ethics*, Spencer's *Synthetic Philosophy*, Montesquieu's *De l'esprit des lois* and Adam Smith's *Wealth of Nations*.[60] He was particularly interested in social Darwinism, an ideology that, given the 'efficiency' of the West, prompted some Chinese intellectuals to express doubts about the 'survival' of their own culture. Yan Fu was impressed by the search for truth and the subordination of the individual for the greater good of society. After reading *A System of Logic* by John Stuart Mill (1806–1873), Yan Fu became one of the first Chinese intellectuals to make clear how thoroughly the encounter with the West was throwing traditional Chinese thought into question:

> [Mill's] insights are as abundant as the threads of silk in a cocoon . . . They will eliminate 80 to 90 per cent of the obsolete patterns of Chinese thought. Applying them will give unimaginable powers to human intelligence.[61]

Since Yan Fu rendered his translations into antiquated classical Chinese, their effect remained limited. From a historical perspective, however, they remain hugely informative. He and other early intermediaries had to contend with countless problems that inevitably accompanied the attempt to make a foreign culture accessible, especially finding the right words for European specialized terms and adequately conveying the underlying concepts. Another problem was having to contend with the terminology that the Japanese had been using for decades in their own appropriation of Western science and philosophy which now, since it had been formulated in Chinese characters, was available for use – an unattractive vision for some Chinese reformers.[62]

TWENTY

Science and Medicine

THE TRANSFORMATION'S DRIVING force would come from elsewhere. Great numbers of students went to Japan, the U.S. and Europe and brought back knowledge and experience which they could apply in their homeland. The classical examinations were abolished in 1905, sealing the fate of the old scholarly class that had constituted the backbone of imperial China's society and bureaucracy for 2,000 years. Inevitably, conflicting forces sought to fill the vacuum left by the increasing irrelevance of the classical scholar-functionaries.

Hu Shi (1891–1962) was one of the first authors of the new era to find a substantial audience. Returning to China after studying in the United States under the philosopher John Dewey, he demanded that colloquial Chinese, which Chinese scholars had long despised and banned from print, should become the country's literary language. His call met with enthusiastic support. From 1920 elementary schools began teaching colloquial Chinese. Within a decade it became the sole form of expression for all levels of Chinese society.[63]

Those returning from the West founded hundreds of new periodicals to spread their ideas of democracy and science throughout the country. In 1907 a group of Chinese exiles established the journal *New World*. Its first issue pointed the way:

The discovery of scientific laws and the expanding wave of revolutions are the marks of mankind in the nineteenth century. The two complement and determine one another, resulting in society's ability to fit in with the laws of nature ... That which was called 'revolution' in the past was nothing but superficial change ... Instead, the revolution of the New Century holds that everything that does not comply with the laws of nature is unwelcome. That is not all, however. The current revolution will be permanent in its effort to approach all that is right and true. Therefore it is now a ruthless and progressive revolution. A revolution that has the happiness of humanity as its goal.[64]

Several statements in this manifesto deserve particular attention. China, the authors wrote, was nothing special in the rivalry of nations or civilizations. It was one location among many in the world in which the all-encompassing revolution was taking place, which would result in the complete hegemony of the sciences. Westerners reading these lines would not notice that the term 'revolution' might mean something different in Chinese from what it means in European languages. In Chinese, revolution translates as *ge ming*, or literally, 'withdrawing the mandate.' Here we meet the same term *ming* – 'mandate' – that we first encountered in the battle cry for existential self-determination: 'I confer the mandate upon myself, heaven does not confer it!' When the readers of *New World* therefore read about 'withdrawing the mandate', for them it was the mandate of past traditions, of their own culture, that was being withdrawn and exchanged for the laws of nature. These would determine how all of humanity would have to behave in the future. This sheds light on why, years later, Hu Shi would look back and write:

> For some three decades now a single name has attained a singular esteem in China; no one, whether educated or not, conservative or progressive, would dare mock it or even just chuckle about it in public. The name is that of 'science'. The value of this honour, which nearly the entire nation recognizes, is another question. But one thing can be said. Since the reform movement began in China, not a single person claiming to be modern would dare to question the importance of science.[65]

Lu Xun (1881–1936), Ba Jin (1904–2005) and many other writers used their influence to spread the 'wave for new thinking' over all of China; all saw Western science as the key to a better future. In 1917 a periodical with the subtitle 'knowledge and science' set a goal of 'enforcing education and a critical view based on truth'. In 1919 students at Beijing University under the direction of Hu Shi founded the journal *New Wave* with the motto of 'acquiring a critical spirit, scientific thinking and a new form of language'. That same year, the publication *Young China* of the 'Association for a Young China' went so far as to accept as members only applicants with no religious affiliation. The list of such developments could continue for pages.

From the very start, Chinese medicine was at the centre of the criticism. That is hardly surprising. Nowhere within a culture are fears and optimism expressed as swiftly and existentially as in the attitudes toward one's own illness. In its more than 2,000-year history, fundamental medical theory has never followed its own dynamic. This kind of dynamic, which one can infer from physicians' experiences and observations, has never existed in either China or Europe. Always, it has been profound social change, the emergence of existential fears within a society and the confidence of finding security in a new order that have changed attitudes toward illness and the order – the health – of an organism.[66]

These contexts are easier to discern in Chinese medical history than in Europe, where, since the time of classical Greece, changes in the prevailing order have taken place more frequently than in China and several social systems have often existed side by side. Stimuli for new ways of looking at the body and its ailments have therefore been rather diffuse. The decline of the Confucian system in the late nineteenth century and its collapse in the twentieth is no exception. The healing arts are always at the cultural centre of civilization. They are at the intersection of religion and nature, economic and social factors, language and technology, and much else. Changes in any one of these aspects will find their expression in medicine. The upheavals in China influenced many of these factors simultaneously. It is hardly surprising, therefore, that Chinese medicine, whose continuity over the previous two millennia had been safeguarded mainly by the congruence of its theories with Confucian social doctrine and the social structures of the Empire, should have then met its end as the dominant approach to healing in China. Initially this had hardly any effects on everyday medical practice. The struggle of the new against the old has always been fought primarily in the minds of intellectuals and political leaders.

The confrontation with Western medicine certainly did not cause the first doubts of the effectiveness of Chinese medicine. Chinese intellectuals had sharply criticized their medical orthodoxy much earlier. This is all the more astonishing as they had no way to compare medical systems and therefore could not point to a better way of healing.

An early example of such criticism is a musical drama from the fifteenth century in which poor training, unscrupulous treatment of patients and greed characterize the two doctors in the story. Since we do not know the author's identity, we cannot tell what (perhaps personal) motivations he may have had to pour such bitter scorn on incompetent doctors.[67] A scholar we do know, Xu Dachun (1693–1771), was more precise in his criticism. He was a polymath whose expertise included medicine, and wrote books on various topics, including several on healing in which he attacked the medical practice of his day. Examples of his opinions include:

'The doctors of today have completely abandoned the good methods of the sages.'

'The tradition of the medical arts has been cut off.'

'Doctors these days do not even know the names of sicknesses.'

'These days the people who select a doctor and those who practice medicine are equally ignorant.'

'The unfounded statements that are fashionable today are not worth being listened to.'

'I sincerely regret that ever since the days of the Tang and the Song, scholars have failed to contribute to the richness of medicine. Instead they have regarded medicine as an unworthy profession. That is why the old traditions have been lost.'[68]

Wang Qingren (1768–1831) was a physician who, after seeing corpses in a cemetery, decided to compare the organs he had observed with primitive drawings of the body's insides that still reflected the antiquated ideas of the thirteenth and fourteenth centuries. He concluded that

> When the ancients discussed the lung, they said the lung had no opening underneath. Why, then, did they write elsewhere that the lung contained holes through which the Qi can enter every storage area? . . . All this is ridiculous nonsense that has been preserved for an eternity . . . Just as they were mistaken about the appearance, they also described the functions incorrectly. Nothing but contradictions and errors.[69]

European literature often suggests that when European medicine was introduced to China, it encountered a medical tradition that had remained intact for 2,000 years at least. Historical documents tell a different story. The intellectual elite (though not the general population) frequently expressed dissatisfaction with the abilities of doctors in general and, more specifically, their professional ethics. When, in the mid-nineteenth century, European medicine was introduced to China on a wider scale primarily by Protestant missionaries, it very rarely met with rejection. European doctors became so popular that some could handle the onslaught of patients only by distributing numbers giving the patients' positions in the queue.

As in other fields in the late nineteenth and early twentieth centuries, some erudite medical theorists tried to achieve a balance between traditional and Western medicine. The attempt failed, as the harsh reckoning with traditional Chinese medicine necessarily had to come from the outside. One especially telling occasion was the so-called Manchurian Plague epidemic of 1910–11. Just as it would do nearly a century later during the SARS epidemic, traditional medicine knew no better remedy than igniting fireworks to drive off the demons supposedly causing the malady. An estimated 60,000 had died before the government appointed a Chinese-born, Cambridge-trained microbiologist named Wu Lien-Teh (1879–1960) to put an end to the scourge.[70]

Wu Lien-Teh was born in Penang, which at the time was part of Britain's Straits Settlements colony, and initially returned there after his studies. Yet despite his education and abilities, he had no opportunity of entering the senior levels of the medical service in Penang. Those positions were reserved for the British colonial elite. Once the Chinese authorities had appointed him to head the fight against the epidemic in Manchuria, his introduction of methods that had long been standard in Europe marked a turning point. Awareness of public health that focused on pathogenic microorganisms had been utterly unknown in China, but soon found political acceptance. In 1916 he became the first president of the China Medical Association and in 1931 was elected director of China's National Quarantine Service.[71]

For the students returning from Japan, the U.S. and Europe, Chinese medicine suddenly looked utterly pathetic. Purely speculative and inspired both in its concepts and terminology by Han-era social structures, it was considered capable of healing only those maladies that modern medicine would hand over to internists. Chinese medicine knew neither surgery nor epidemiology. It had a vague idea of microorganisms that could cause illness, but its theory did not include such possibilities. Mental illness was hardly acknowledged. Most importantly, however, Chinese medicine lacked the very element which by that time had elevated European healing above all other systems of medical theory and practice: going beyond the individual's own responsibility for illness and taking living and working conditions into account. The individual can do little to change them, which is why responsibility for them lies with society in general, and healthcare policy in particular. This was where the real strength of European medicine lay, and where attentive observers noted that Chinese traditions of healing had nothing to offer.

The practitioners of traditional medicine, who were understandably interested in maintaining their positions, made no effort to improve matters. As a result, China's leading writers exposed the deficiencies of traditional medicine in their novels. Their messages were essentially identical. Medicine was there to cure and possibly to prevent disease. Chinese medicine, they asserted, was the disease of China itself. Instead of easing discomfort, it caused added suffering. The authors did not have to search long for examples of the incompetence of Chinese healing. Yu Yue (1821–1907), whom today's supporters of traditional Chinese medicine regard as their first and worst enemy, based his work 'On Eliminating Chinese Medicine' (1890) on the deaths of his wife and children.

Lu Xun, the outstanding writer of the early twentieth century, had begun his studies at the Jiangnan Naval Academy when 'the harm that ignorant, old-fashioned doctors caused' prompted him to study Western medicine in Japan. He soon recognized, however, that the pen gave him better opportunities than the scalpel to heal his compatriots of their sicknesses. In his short stories he repeatedly discussed the problem of a traditional medicine that not only fails to heal but causes additional harm. Among the best known of these was the story titled 'Medicine' (*Yao*, 1919), which explores the death of a child from absurd medications and the suffering of its mother.[72]

Like Yu Yue, Lu Xun could write about such matters from personal experience. His story 'Father's Illness', written in 1926, is autobiographical. The novel *Family* by Ba Jin, another well-known author of the time, had a similar background, as did the story 'Grandmother Decides' by Lao She (1899–1966). When Zhang Shichuan, an early Chinese film director, finally decided to make the first American-style slapstick comedy in China in 1922, his choice of an object of ridicule that the whole audience could grasp was an easy one. The lead role in 'The Fruit Seller's Love' was a doctor of traditional Chinese medicine, portrayed just as the director believed the audience saw members of the profession: unscrupulous, incompetent and hopelessly entangled in the values of the past. The result was a good laugh for everyone.

Initially European medicine did little to emphasize its superiority to the Chinese tradition. The first physicians to arrive in China with the British East India Company in the early nineteenth century certainly did not act presumptuously. When J. Livingstone came to Macao in 1820 he immediately sought contact with his Chinese counterparts. Soon afterwards, Thomas R. Colledge also opened his ophthalmology office in Macao. However, his practice quickly made apparent how different his available therapies were from those of Chinese doctors. Couching, a primitive form of surgery to treat cataracts, was introduced to China from India in the eighth century, but remained a marginal procedure. Traditional Chinese medical theory was simply incapable of accepting any such therapeutic technique. Chinese medical practice never accepted couching, let alone developed it further. One can imagine, then, that demand for eye operations at Colledge's clinic was high. Once he had himself painted standing proudly next to a patient, as an avid young Chinese intern stands ready to give the woman her eyesight back.

There were very deliberate limits set on the Westerners' readiness to help, however. When Protestant, and later, Catholic U.S. missionaries who were also trained doctors were sent to China, they were always under explicit instructions not to use their medical skills for the benefit of the natives. They had received medical training to improve their own survival chances, which in the early nineteenth century were not great.[73] Still, the missionaries swiftly recognized that with their healing arts they possessed a far more effective means of attracting the Chinese than their religious teachings, which sounded thoroughly outlandish to Chinese ears. Some missionaries devised elaborate strategies, blending medical diagnosis and therapy with proselytizing in order to improve the results of their version of pastoral care. An earnest dispute also erupted over whether training Chinese students was worthwhile. Some missionaries suspected that doing so would result in Chinese people going to their own Western medical doctors instead of to the mission practices.

The standing orders of the parent organizations in the U.S. to attend to the souls of the Chinese and not their bodies were combined with very paltry funding.[74] In the first two decades of their existence, therefore, the mission clinics presented a woeful picture that was far removed from the standards of hospitals in the United States at that time. As late as 1920 the China Medical Missionary Association reported that 92 per cent of the clinics had to get by without a fresh water supply; 73 per cent had no possibility of sterilizing bed sheets; 50 per cent bathed their patients infrequently, if at all; 34 per cent operated without autoclaves to sterilize bandages; 31 per cent had no laboratory; 82 per cent no incubators for bacteria; and 87 per cent no x-ray machine.[75] This changed only once those who had returned from Japan and the u.s. raised a storm of indignation with their reports of what Western medicine was really like and how the missionaries had deceived the people. Even before the outbreak of the Great War, the Rockefeller Foundation saw a need to establish modern hospitals in China on a level with Johns Hopkins University Hospital – the gold standard of the time – as a 'showcase' of Western medicine. The project would only produce results – delayed by the war – in 1921, with the founding of the Union Medical Hospitals in five Chinese cities, and especially the still-elite Peking Union Medical College, which then set the standard in China for providing modern medical training in English.

TWENTY-ONE

How much Westernization?

THE ESTABLISHMENT OF these visible acknowledgements of Western scientific and medical superiority coincided with the beginning of the last great debate over how defensible all this Westernization was. As people in China had comprehended, everything that made the West so superior rested on modern science. Western readers may regard the many calls to adopt the sciences as the measure of all things in China as an obvious con-sequence of rejecting the relationist interpretation of nature, as expressed in the Yin-Yang and Five Phases doctrines, in favour of chemistry, physics, biology and so on. That was certainly how many Chinese people returning from universities in the U.S. and Europe regarded the matter. Yet more than a handful of the reformers saw that achieving this intellectual *volte-face* would hardly be as simple as it appeared on paper.

In fact it proved enormously difficult to part company with the relationist view of society and nature that had been held for 2,000 years. Just imagine how Western culture would have reacted if it had suddenly encountered some other civilization that, with a completely different view of the world, rendered obsolete all the knowledge and technological triumphs attained through physics and chemistry while giving rise to other, wondrous things that physicists and chemists were at a loss to explain. A centuries-long process of development linked with many famous names would suddenly become irrelevant. All the many great works these authors wrote, all their Nobel Prizes, would suddenly become so much waste paper and scrap metal. Inconceivable? Indeed!

Yet this was precisely the reality facing the inheritors of a 2,000-year-old doctrine of the systematic correspondence of all things. All at once, the many thousands of writings which they believed represented the pinnacles of scholarship seemed no longer to mean anything at all.[76] For both conservatives and 'modern people', as Hu Shi called them, who decided that the natural sciences were indispensable, the approach that had slowly emerged in Europe through centuries of conflict with religion and speculation and which recognized only facts and objectively verifiable truths was completely alien.

The term for the new approach to interpreting and influencing the world was *ke xue*, which was probably coined in Japan and reached China from there. *Ke* means 'field' or 'subject'. A *ke xue* is a 'doctrinal structure divided into fields'. Just how thin the concept was that arrived in China via this term is shown by the definition offered by Ding Wenjiang (1887–1936), a proponent of the 'scientification' of Chinese society.[77] Scientific method, he wrote, is

> nothing other than the ordering of all natural information into various classes and finding the order in which all these are arranged. After these have been arranged into classes and their order has been determined, we use the simplest and simultaneously clearest language to summarize everything, and can then call this a universal law of science.[78]

In discussions with Chinese people who believe that the use of Chinese medicine is still justified, one frequently hears the argument that this kind of medicine is thoroughly founded in 'natural sciences' – a contention that practically begs to be disputed. In his or her own language, a Chinese person would of course say something completely different. This medicine is very much a 'doctrinal structure divided into departments', *ke xue*, for example *fu ke*, *er ke*, *shang ke*, *nei ke* and so on, meaning the medicinal fields dealing with women, children, injuries and internal medicine, to name only a few. Hearing it described like this, one can only agree with the speaker. The term *ke xue* means very little. In fact, it will not be associated with the European idea of 'science' at all unless the person hearing it has had solid training in European intellectual history. And who had that in early twentieth-century China?

The spokesmen in the science debate included both Ding Wenjiang and Hu Shi, who advocated completely adopting Western science and culture, Zhang Junmai (1887–1969), also known as Carsun Chang, and Liang Shuming (1893–1988),[79] who supported a more superficial appropriation of Western science.[80] For the latter group, holding on to traditional Chinese moral philosophy was essential, as the natural sciences, or 'doctrinal structure divided into fields' of the West, could never sufficiently explain the more sophisticated, metaphysical aspects of existence. Carsun Chang pointed out the contradictions between subjectivity, intuition, a relationist (or synthetic) view of the world, free will and the uniqueness of each person as characteristics of a life philosophy on the one hand, and believing the laws of causality and accepting the uniformity of all phenomena in the universe as the central concepts of natural science on the other. He declared that these two approaches were irreconcilable and that the natural sciences could never produce a philosophy of life.[81]

European philosophers engaged in a comparable discussion at the time. The protagonists of China's science debate quoted Kant as well as importing the ideas of contemporary thinkers including John Dewey, Henri Bergson, Bertrand Russell, Rudolf Eucken and Hans Driesch to China.[82] The dispute centred on the concepts 'natural science' vs 'philosophy of life' and matter vs mind and soul, and brought ideas from sceptical idealism, phenomenology, monism, pluralism and other European movements. Sometimes it became abrasive, for example when Ding Wenjiang condemned his opponents as 'reincarnated ghosts of Western and Chinese metaphysics.'

Some conservatives favourably contrasted the philanthropic morals of the relationist world-view with the cold, analytical approach of Western science. Such morals were no use, responded advocates of scientism (comprehensive applicability of the natural sciences), pointing out that through the centuries and despite their allegedly philanthropic morality, the Chinese had continually slaughtered each other on a grand scale. 'Zhang Xianzhong alone butchered more people in Sichuan than those killed in the World War, to say nothing of the atrocities of the Manchus in some southern provinces. We would do well to ask ourselves what all this intellectual civilization has cost us', wrote Ding Wenjiang.[83]

The debate over the value of the more 'intellectual civilization' of the East compared with the West's 'materialist civilization' continued for several years. It drew in nearly all of China's notable intellectuals of the time before leaving most with the realization that there was no way to deny the centrality of the natural sciences. The evidence that scientific objectivity produced more than individualized intuition and speculation became more and more overwhelming.[84]

In addition, the efforts of some Chinese intellectuals that even today have not completely ended, known as 'sciences with a regional character' (*difanxing kexue*), which tried to at least relativize, if not to halt, the triumphant success of 'Western' science, remained only marginally significant. [85]

Looking back, one is struck by the seriousness of all those who participated in this debate. It was about far more than a little modernization. It was about the fundamental question that a culture under pressure from another that is superior, at least technologically and militarily, must ask itself: how can we ward off the danger and return to our old greatness? Where did any comparable process take place among the non-European cultures that felt provoked by Western values and superiority? Responding to this superiority and to the waning influence of traditional values by resorting to terrorism and calling for collective hatred was never even considered in China.

TWENTY-TWO

Marxism in China

ONE IMPORTANT VOICE of that time has yet to be named: that of Chen Duxiu (1879–1942), a co-founder and, from 1921, the first General Secretary of the Communist Party of China. The question 'To what extent can individuals influence the course of events?' is asked practically every time people think about history. Are the individuals whose decisions and actions we associate with historical developments really the causes of these developments, or are there other reasons why, during a given period of change, this or that person rose to forge the political transformations with which they are forever after personally identified? Without a doubt, Chen Duxiu and Mao Zedong (1893–1976) are two personalities who justify this question.

Chen Duxiu came from a wealthy family of the old Confucian upper class. Since his father died shortly after Chen was born, his upbringing was left to his grandfather, who was known to enforce his ideas of childrearing using a whip. Here one might see the personal trauma that followed Chen Duxiu for his whole life in his embittered struggle against China's traditional culture. The pain he suffered personally complemented the injuries the imperial powers inflicted on China. The fact that his grandfather also observed superficial formalities (in Chen Duxiu's opinion) such as cleanliness and etiquette while indulging in what his grandson considered a depraved addiction to opium only completed the grandfather's symbolic representation of the old order that the young man detested.

In his youth Chen passed the imperial examinations with the best marks in his province. A few years later, while sitting in one of the little booths in which candidates for the civil services were tested, the entire system had come to disgust him so thoroughly that after a few hours he left, without having taken the exam, to devote his life to paving the way for a 'new' China. In 1900 he travelled to Tokyo to study and came into contact with nationalist and revolutionary Chinese student groups there. He was disgusted by the racist slurs of the revolutionary theorist and subsequent founder of the Republic of China, Sun Yatsen, whose arguments for abolishing the alien Manchu rule in China included the assertion that the Manchu were inferior to the Chinese race. Chen Duxiu's political stance at the time is now generally considered that of a social democrat, which meant he probably found few sympathizers in the seething atmosphere of Chinese students and exiles in Tokyo.

In 1907 Chen Duxiu travelled to Paris, where many Chinese students and revolutionaries lived at the time. His encounter with French culture and political life was a revelation. Here, at a stroke, he believed he could see all that was needed for a better future for China: democracy, which he encountered through the writings of Lafayette and Seignobos; evolutionary theory as rendered by Lamarck; and socialism, as espoused in the writings of Babeuf, Saint-Simon and Fourier. His love of France turned into a profound aversion after the Treaty of Versailles, which handed Germany's territories in China to Japan instead of returning them, was signed in 1919.

Yet disillusionment was not the only reason why Chen Duxiu and others began to revise their opinions of the West. They decided that imperialism had triumphed over the rights of nations. The Western powers had engaged in four years of unprecedented slaughter and material destruction. The many Western philosophers invited to China to shed light on the differences between the ascendant civilization of the West and China's prostrated and possibly doomed culture were generally at a loss to explain this debacle and frequently declared that the catastrophe of the First World War was the West's declaration of moral bankruptcy. There was one exception, however. The Marxists offered reasons for both the contradictions that had led to the war and the fundamental causes for China's humiliation. They also offered a promising way to remedy at least the latter of these evils.

Marxism, then, was the second great European intellectual construct after the 'natural sciences' that some intellectuals prescribed to Chinese society. Neither had roots in Chinese society. Chen Duxiu made his life's work out of banishing his personal traumas by overcoming the traumas his country had suffered and continued to suffer. To him, combining these two 'treatments' seemed to be the most effective medicine.

By now it should come as no surprise that Marxism, like the idea of science, did not arrive in China in the way it had been conceived in Europe. The intellectual and socio-economic circumstances were simply too different. However, to trace the creative reception – that is, the process of adjustment to the receiving culture – that Marxism encountered in China, we must return to the social and democratic developments in Europe that began in the late eighteenth century. These developments helped to greatly strengthen Europe and temporarily gave this relatively small corner of the earth a level of influence in the world that far exceeded its size. Yet they also spawned an element of political thought and action that now works in the exact opposite direction. It cemented the politically justified concerns of social welfare with the destructive powers of envy. The emotion of envy is probably a legacy from prehistoric times, when smaller groups of people living together knew that 'nature' was responsible for distributing the essentials of life, and that it provided more or less the same quantity of food year on year. In its origins, then, envy is inextricably bound with the ideal of a small, unified community of individuals with the same rights.

When solidarity characterizes a community, each member knows that all depend on one another and that available resources must be fairly shared. When one member accumulates resources, the assumption must be that others consequently lack them. The result is an imbalance and a sense of injustice that A has more and B less. Envy seeks to take away from others that which distinguishes them from the rest of the crowd. It has no beneficial functions. Envy is among the most destructive of the broad spectrum of human emotions.

In very few societies is envy insignificant in the presence of those who are better off. For many years, the u.s. was one. The cake seemed infinitely large and all could help themselves. Those who seized their chance could literally go from dishwasher to millionaire. Instead of being envious of the rich, people felt regret or, at the most, castigated themselves for not having used this or that opportunity. This attitude is expressed in the Chinese adage *wo ming zai wo* – roughly, 'Every man forges his own destiny.'

Strikingly, China has traditionally known hardly any strategies to reverse excessive ownership or render it invisible. Only the concept of the *gu* demon fulfilled this role. Anyone who suddenly became wealthy, it was believed, had probably allied himself with the *gu* demon, which required a human host. When a person helped the *gu* demon to find such a host, the demon rewarded his helper by giving him the host's entire fortune. The involuntary host paid for his new function with his life. No other crime carried such draconian punishment in China. The alleged offender was subjected to a gruesome execution; then his entire family was extinguished. Yet such cases remained isolated incidents. Chinese society was never infected by a *gu* hysteria, as it was – and sometimes still is – in places where the evil eye, *mal ojo* and other ideas influence everyday life. These ideas have grown from fear of those who could demonstrate the destructive power of envy.

Marxism declared itself the advocate of the losers of the capitalist-industrial revolution, then the victims of colonialism and other aftereffects of capitalism. In doing so its originators – certainly unintentionally – made the emotion of envy philosophically and politically respectable, probably for the first time in history. The cause of the 'disadvantaged', 'oppressed', 'underprivileged' or 'exploited' brings the image of a closed community in solidarity back into focus and apportions the blame for these peoples' suffering to those who are better off. In some respects, decrying this direct causality is certainly justified; but what policy should one follow as a result?

Marxism is driven by envy and is neither social nor democratic whenever, in political reality, it is fixated solely on the class struggle – that is, the destruction of one's adversary. Just like old-fashioned envy, it has no realistic, constructive alternatives to offer. That the objective of a dictatorship of the proletariat could grow from these foundations – Lenin's and Stalin's murderous machinery with its many millions of victims and other collateral damage, as well as inhumane regimes that subjugated much of the Eurasian continent for decades – must be seen as the triumph of envy. The demise of all economies built on this ideology simultaneously laid bare the nature of those base emotions that, alongside sophisticated social theories, constituted the foundation of Marxism.

To be broadly successful, whether in Europe or China, an ideology of Marxism's stripe needs to be attractive in at least two ways: it must persuade the intellect and appeal to populist impulses. Some adherents might feel drawn by both the idea's intellectual and populist sides, but they are probably the exception. The intellectual attractiveness of Marxism functions on several levels, some of which came from older European modes of thought; others originated in the works of Marx and Engels. The ideas of dialectical materialism and the materialist-economic determinants of historical progress, radical criticism of religion, the idea of capital fetishism, the vision of an exit from the cycles of exploitation and so on mostly offered new analytical instruments for understanding and perhaps remedying the many disconcerting and shameful effects of industrialization and the dominance of national and international capital.

Yet such intellectual constructs cannot by themselves reach the greater masses of people, let alone galvanize them. For that one needs the populist element, the persuasive power of the more easily understood argument that dark forces – in the guise of capitalists and their institutions – deprive other people of that which they deserve. This view gives rise to the class of the exploited. The dark forces must be identified and unmasked, and that which they have wrongly taken from others must be restored to the dispossessed.

Of these two levels of argument, in China the purely intellectual, theoretical formulations were new. The forms of ownership that Marx and Engels analysed did not exist in China.
Calls to expropriate – if not to eliminate – the proprietary and
affluent classes were also new there. It had never been politically
opportune in China to pay attention to the welfare of the masses.
The ideals of Confucianism, such as the demand for proper
interpersonal behaviour, were aimed always at the individual
and held practically no relevance for greater society or indeed
state policy. The idea of compassion that Buddhism had
introduced in China likewise failed to gain much influence.

Also, China had never broadly known communities in solidarity beyond that of the family, certain religious associations
or secret societies – despite some Confucian recommendations
that could be interpreted to that effect. Solidarity can emerge
only from an awareness of belonging to a community in which
each depends on the other. This consciousness could unfold at
the national level within European nation-states in the nineteenth and early twentieth centuries as an effect of competition
among these nation-states. It also led to real political achievements, for example in the advent of health insurance and retirement pensions, before waning in the increasingly multicultural
and heterogeneous societies of the latter twentieth century.[86]
China was simply too big and too diverse in its social fabric to
ever see the rise of a sense of community that spanned the strata
of society. The consciousness that was and remains predominant
in China is that the fate of the individual lies in his or her own
hands.[87] This kind of view obstructs awareness of the overall
situation in society of which the individual's living conditions
are a part. European references to social conditions as variable
constants were therefore a revelation for Chinese intellectuals,
who had never experienced any comparable ideas.

The intellectuals among the revolutionaries adopted
practically every concept of Marxist theory. Besides anti-
imperialism it was especially the atheistic and pro-scientific
(that is, materialistic) content that grew in influence. The view
of the great landowners or magnates as sharing responsibility

for the misery of hundreds of thousands of impoverished peasants justified the class struggle and the demands, if not to physically eradicate this class, then to abolish it and its power once and for all.

The sole aspect that never gained a real foothold in China was the part of this ideology that grew into a general attitude in Europe. The discovery of social welfare gave rise to political voices who spread the idea among their clientele that the individual's real or alleged plight could be attributable only to others' aggrandizement. From this foundation they derived a belief that they did not have to do anything to improve their own living conditions; that was the responsibility, indeed, the duty, of the well off. This mentality was so alien to the Chinese tradition that it has never existed in the Chinese reception of Marxism. Chinese intellectuals adapted Marxism to their own needs and used it as a tool to forge a new social order. Unlike their Western neighbours all the way to East Berlin, they did not subscribe to the illusion that this ideology would suffice to create flourishing landscapes. The reforms of Deng Xiaoping were marked by an 'I am responsible for my own fate' pragmatism that is no longer conceivable in Europe.

Chen Duxiu's incremental turn to Marxism reflected the motives that steered many of his peers onto similar paths. Certainly, however, Chen Duxiu is regarded as the most 'destructive' critic of the old China and a strident advocate of realigning the country along scientific principles. His twofold ordeal, first from the suffering his grandfather, a representative of the old Confucian order, inflicted on him, and second from Western aggression against his country in general, probably determined his radicalism.

The mouthpiece for Chen Duxiu and other more or less like-minded people, including Hu Shi and Lu Xun, became the journal *New Youth*, which Chen founded in 1915. Initially guided by social democratic ideas, then increasingly influenced by materialist views of history and society, Chen Duxiu led the call to abandon Confucian tradition and rejuvenate China through science. Other reformers such as Kang Youwei (1858–1927) recognized China's deficiencies and demanded many reforms within the system; for example, saying that Confucianism should be elevated to the status of state religion. The atheist Chen Duxiu, meanwhile, rejected all forms of religious speculation. 'Democracy in politics, science in ideas', was his best-known slogan.

The first issue of *New Youth* included a 'solemn appeal to youth' that exhorted China's emerging generation to finally discard the Chinese tradition of being 'young in years but old in the mind'. He based his arguments on the Utilitarian ideas of British philosopher John Stuart Mill and saw his views confirmed by the Positivism of Auguste Comte. The task of the twentieth-century economic philosopher, Chen wrote, must be to meet the requirements of the time, turn away from analytical approaches and instead 'become a prophetic thinker who brings all branches of thought together'. Statements like this make clear that, despite his unrestricted rhetorical dedication to modern sciences, Chen Duxiu retained at least elements of his country's synthetic-relationist intellectual heritage.

Chen's analysis of Germany also demonstrates that contacts with Western idiosyncrasies remained too brief and superficial to properly comprehend the West and its foundations. Germany, he wrote, was an outstanding example of putting scientific progress at the service of the very highest kind of materialistic civilization. Everything formalistic, imaginary and useless in everyday life had to be excised. In cutting words he expressed his contempt for traditional Chinese scholars and their knowledge, taking some digs at traditional medicine along the way:

> Our scholars understand nothing about science, so they help themselves with Yin-Yang symbols and belief in the Five Phases of Change to confuse the world and mislead the people . . .
>
> Our doctors understand nothing about science; they know nothing about human anatomy and have no idea how to analyse medicine. They have never even heard of bacterial poisonings and infections . . .

The pinnacle of their quaint illusions is the theory of *qi*, which in reality belongs in the repertoire of professional jugglers and Daoist priests. We will never find this *qi*, even if we search the entire universe for it. All these imaginative ideas and fanciful faiths can be corrected from the bottom up by science, because to uncover truth by using science we must verify everything with facts.

The amount of truth in the universe is unlimited and the productive regions in the realm of the natural sciences waiting for pioneering work are enormous. Young people, get to work!

When one considers how many young people in Europe and America these days, whether conventional doctors or alternative practitioners, spend many thousands of dollars and euros on receiving training in the traditional Chinese perspective that was so reviled, and with what hastiness a form of healing based on this perspective is being included in the curricula of Western academic institutions, one can only marvel at this remarkable spectacle of transcultural give-and-take.

Increasingly espousing a strict materialism that interpreted all reality as 'matter in movement', Chen Duxiu finally trans-ferred the laws of science to the social sciences. The bridge, he wrote, was economics. Culture, religion, ethics, education – all these facets of civilization were comprehensible only by under-standing their economic foundations. Therefore there could be no sense in changing culture, religion, ethics or education. If one wanted to change society, one had to change its economic foundations. The laws of economics are the regulatory forces that determine all else, he wrote. These beliefs already put Chen Duxiu in the intellectual vicinity of Marxism. That ideology would only gain influence in China after the conclusion of the Treaty of Versailles that outraged the Chinese, however, as Germany's possessions in Shandong were handed over to Japan in violation of all principles of national self-determination – and the success of the Bolshevik Revolution in Russia.

Although its analysis was directed at early industrial Western Europe, Marxism proved to be the ideal alternative to China's traditional social doctrines and structures. It glorified science as the basis of modern society and saw itself as the complementary social science, based on materialism, of the natural sciences that are themselves founded in materialism. Moreover, Marxism was a Western ideology and therefore was a priori imbued with the glow of progress. It was also a theory that promised to help throw off the yoke of imperialism. Yet again, an opportunity had been found to defeat the barbarians with their own weapons – this time figuratively.

TWENTY-THREE

The Path to the Present

LENIN'S THESIS, STATING that imperialism was the final phase of capitalism from which socialism would necessarily follow, left some Chinese revolutionaries doubting whether China, which had not progressed to the stage of capitalism, could itself establish socialism. This was the spirit in which the founder of the republic, Sun Yatsen, demanded as late as 1923 that China must achieve national unity and independence before working towards the goal of a socialist society. The augmentation of Marxism by Leninism did not result in a new doctrine that could be applied to the Chinese situation conveniently and without alteration. Discussion within the fledgling Communist Party, which had few members compared to the republican People's Party (*Guomindang*) of Sun Yatsen but many conflicting opinions, centred on finding China's place within the global revolution.

Anarchism, especially in the writings of the Russian geographer and social revolutionary Pyotr Kropotkin (1842–1921), found widespread support. Kropotkin was among those who took the idea of harnessing science for society to a new extreme. By using science, humanity could be in a position to directly influence its natural environment and control the direction of biological evolution, he wrote. Yet his anarchist ideas impaired the effectiveness of science, since Kropotkin said that just as the individual loses his political autonomy and awareness by ceding power to representatives, he must also lose his innate understanding of nature and natural inventiveness once scientific inquiry is handed over to specialists.

The discrepancy between the internationalism of the Communists and the nationalist aspirations of many Chinese reformers likewise facilitated the emergence of factions. Practically every effort to decide policy exposed ideological fault-lines. At the outset, in 1921, the Communist International (Comintern) advised the CPC to join forces with the Guomindang. The Second Party Congress in 1922 resolved to first achieve a nationalist, bourgeois-democratic revolution in which the industrial proletariat (which then hardly existed in China) would ally itself with the peasants. The bourgeoisie – whoever that term denoted in China at the time – would be overthrown at a later time, to be replaced by a dictatorship of workers and farmers.[88] The Communist Party's internal disarray reflected the political turmoil throughout China which did not significantly subside until 1927. That year, a republican central government worthy of the name was finally established, and the Guomindang leadership felt sufficiently in control to purge the Communists in the unloved alliance once and for all through massacres in Shanghai and elsewhere. Thousands were killed.

Chen Duxiu had repeatedly advocated dissolving the united front with the republicans but was overruled by his comrades, who had come under pressure from the Comintern. Nonetheless the disastrous end of the alliance in 1927 was blamed on Chen Duxiu. The first General Secretary of the CPC, sometimes called 'China's Lenin', lost his party office and, two years later, was expelled from the party altogether. A second, temporary coalition between China's two great political camps in the struggle against Japan and the ensuing break after the Second World War that led to civil war finally ended in 1949 with the Communist victory and the founding of the People's Republic of China.

There were many reasons for the Communist triumph. It would probably have never come, however, had Mao Zedong (1893–1976), an early associate of Chen Duxiu and from 1945 Chairman of the Central Committee – that is, the leader of the CPC – not committed himself to a variant of Communist revolution appropriate to China, thereby accepting the risk of temporary banishment by his party. Contrary to the position of the Comintern, Mao – who came from an agricultural family – saw the peasants as the only force in China capable of carrying out a revolution, and recognized the need to build up a guerilla force based in the countryside that would be far harder to fight than a traditional standing army. This strategy demonstrated its value in the long fight against the Japanese. The price was very high, since the Japanese responded with unimaginable brutality. Whenever the Japanese attacked the Communist guerilla bases, they eradicated the entire civilian population, leaving practically no-one alive in their wake.

Even amid the greatest hardships, Mao Zedong never lost sight of the actual goal of returning China to international power and esteem with the help of 'science' while cutting the country's dependence on foreign powers. He expressed his belief in the efficacy of Marxism as a science of society in 1940 in the following words, which anticipate the 'war against nature' of the 1950s and '60s that would accompany the attacks on the 'class enemies' within the party's own ranks. They also foreshadow Mao's loosening grip on reality during his later decades.

For the purpose of attaining freedom in society, man must use social science to understand and change society and carry out social revolution. For the purpose of attaining freedom in the world of nature, man must use natural science to understand, conquer and change nature and thus attain freedom from nature.[89]

That same year, Mao also clearly presented to the party his ideas about China's future 'new-democratic culture':

New-democratic culture is national. It opposes imperialist oppression and upholds the dignity and independence of the Chinese nation. It belongs to our own nation and bears our own national characteristics. It links up with the socialist and new-democratic cultures of all other nations and they are related in such a way that they can absorb something from each other and help each other to develop, together forming a new world culture; but as a revolutionary national culture it can never link up with any reactionary imperialist culture of whatever nation. To nourish her own culture China needs to assimilate a good deal of foreign progressive culture, not enough of which was done in the past.

We should assimilate whatever is useful to us today not only from the present-day socialist and new-democratic cultures but also from the earlier cultures of other nations, for example, from the culture of the various capitalist countries in the Age of Enlightenment. However, we should not gulp any of this foreign material down uncritically, but must treat it as we do our food – first chewing it, then submitting it to the working of the stomach and intestines with their juices and secretions, and separating it into nutriment to be absorbed and waste matter to be discarded – before it can nourish us.

To advocate wholesale Westernization is wrong. China has suffered a great deal from the mechanical absorption of foreign material. Similarly, in applying Marxism to China, Chinese Communists must fully and properly integrate the universal truth of Marxism with the concrete practice of the Chinese revolution, or in other words, the universal truth of Marxism must be combined with specific national characteristics and acquire a definite national form if it is to be useful, and in no circumstances can it be applied subjectively as a mere formula.

Marxists who make a fetish of formulas are simply playing the fool with Marxism and the Chinese revolution, and there is no room for them in the ranks of the Chinese revolution. Chinese culture should have its own form, its own national form. National in form and new-democratic in content – such is our new culture today.

New-democratic culture is scientific. Opposed as it is to all feudal and superstitious ideas, it stands for seeking truth from facts, for objective truth and for the unity of theory and practice.[90]

China has had several options available since the late nineteenth century of how to respond to the trauma that the Western powers had inflicted on the country. These remarks of Mao Zedong contain all the core elements of the approach that would eventually return China to greatness: unflinchingly exposing the deficiencies of one's own culture and, discarding all taboos, adopting those aspects of European culture that China needed to return to the world stage. Mao's words make clear what many before him had failed to express elegantly: the key was the right preparation of this regimen, making it digestible by China and therefore nourishing for that organism.

What these remarks do not yet indicate are the huge barriers that would obstruct the path of introducing modern science and the technologies and medical practices derived from it for twenty years after the founding of the People's Republic. In some ways the consequences would be onerous; in others, disastrous.

Excited by the success of the revolution and China's 'liberation', many highly trained Chinese scientists returned to their homelands from the West to join in the effort of building up the new China. Within a few years, their enthusiasm for working for their country on home soil would, in the great majority of cases, turn to bitter disappointment.

In 1938 the rector of Heidelberg University personally wrote a letter to chemistry student Wilhelm Mann, banning him as a Jew from ever again entering the university buildings. Mann sought refuge in Shanghai, worked for the Chinese Red Cross during the war in Guiyang in the country's interior, and completed his studies after 1945 at St John's University in Shanghai. Afterwards, he worked for twenty years as a biochemist at the Academy of Sciences in Shanghai where, in 1966, he again found himself as isolated in his laboratory as he had been in 1938 in Heidelberg. He applied for a visa to East Germany; in East Berlin he continued working in his field.

During the 1950s and '60s Mann witnessed his colleagues' enthusiasm for applying the knowledge they had gained in the West to conduct the right scientific research for their country and its needs. Initially they had access to only basic technology but kept a scientific library that always stayed abreast of the latest advances.

These efforts increasingly came into conflict with the priorities of the Communist ideologues. The reception of the work of

Soviet agronomist Trofim Lysenko proved to be a particularly disastrous error. Lysenko epitomized the hubristic idea so prevalent in the Marxist camp that society and nature could be transformed within short periods of time to better serve the needs of humanity. According to exponents of 'Lysenkoism', the 'passive' stance of Mendelian genetics, along with other areas of 'Western' science, was nothing more than an expression of 'bourgeois idealism'. Such passivity could not be reconciled with the Marxist ambition of steering society and even nature. It was the latest incarnation of Ge Hong's old cry of 'I, and not heaven, am responsible for my fate!' For Ge Hong, the elixir of long life was the sole escape from the limits on human existence fixed by 'heaven'. For the Marxists, the modern sciences presented an incomparably broader foundation on which to fight the 'war against nature'. Lysenkoism went so far as to promise not only passive comprehension of natural processes but swift, proactive change. It was the promise of rapidly creating new biological species and solving problems such as food shortages that opened many doors for that Soviet scientist.

In retrospect these expectations proved to be scientific and agricultural dead ends. Passing judgement is easy, but one must put oneself in the context of the time: a period of rapid change. Party ideologues who as a rule had no understanding of 'natural science' in particular or science in general searched for ways to reconcile their theories with the reality of founding a state and building up a socialist society. Many questions were weighed up. How dependent, if at all, should one be on foreigners? What balance should there be between basic science and research on the one hand and applied science on the other? What relationship should natural science experts and representatives of revolutionary egalitarian ideology have? What about subsidies for science and progress? According to Mann, however, the most important thing of all was the spirit of enthusiasm and selflessness that scientists around him felt in those early years towards the arduous tasks they faced, which, they believed, would result in a better world. Cut off from supplies of essential laboratory equipment and chemicals, they nonetheless sought great achievements. Under these conditions, uncovering the structure of insulin and synthesizing this enzyme were astonishing achievements.

Among the ideologues, meanwhile, the idea took hold that 'popular science' had to be established. The fact that Lysenkoism could gain respectability over the objections of scientists trained in the West was due partly to the Soviet Union's canonization as a role model and the often brutal consequences that Western-trained scientists faced for making critical remarks. The influence that Kropotkin had exerted three decades earlier on Chinese reformers also still showed its effects. They now saw their visions confirmed. With his 'transformist' theories of human power over the development of natural processes, Kropotkin both anticipated Lysenko and warned against entrusting scientific creativity to scientific experts. Every important discovery in the past came from people who were first and foremost practitioners, he wrote.[91]

It was in doctrines like these that the ideologues of the Great Leap Forward and other movements of the 1950s and '60s saw their justification in condemning as bourgeois those Western-trained scientists who worked according to Western scientific methods, especially in basic research. They disqualified these scientists as harmful to socialist society and demanded a science in their place that was truly committed to dialectics and materialism. Old arguments from the 1930s were taken up again here. At that time the CPC had criticized the promotion of science under Sun Yatsen's Guomindang party as a cover for nurturing an intelligentsia of experts and technocrats with a direct connection to the capitalist, counter-revolutionary and bourgeois West, thereby obstructing the social revolution they believed was essential for China.[92]

These debates and dynamics were all reflected within the microcosm of the Academy of Sciences laboratory where Wilhelm Mann worked. Attempts to train lab assistants to become serious scientists in the shortest time possible, as ordered by Mao Zedong, ultimately failed. Lysenkoism was forcibly implemented under Soviet influence. These episodes and assessments of how they affected daily work in the lab are all vividly recounted in Wilhelm Mann's memoirs:

Lysenkoists came to Shanghai to give lectures. They came from the Soviet Union. And we were officially notified that the environment, not the gene, was the decisive thing. It was all portrayed as if classical genetics was something very reactionary and therefore had to be rejected. Because it was the environment that was decisive, not heredity. And we were instructed ahead of time not to ask any stupid questions, because it would not have taken much effort to knock them down. We were told to simply listen quietly. The institute's directors said so. They knew themselves that it was all hogwash, but could do nothing against it. As a result, no one worked on genetics any more – for years. Because either they would have had to produce nonsense, just like Lysenko, or they would have been told that they were against Lysenko and against the Soviet Union, meaning counterrevolutionary. Then they would have been removed from the institute.

We did genetic research in plant physiology using corn. That was a popular object of genetics at the time. Then, someone from the u.s. who had done bacterial genetics came to us. Then he didn't do any more genetics. We discussed modern molecular genetics in biology at length. We also spoke about [Jacques] Monod and [François] Jacob, that model was very current at the time. But no work was done, nothing.

By then there was sufficient data, including in the Soviet Union, that the theories of Lysenko were absurd and practically impossible to comprehend. One student of Lysenko, a woman named Lebeshinskaya, had even ground up cells and claimed she could produce living cells again through incubation. That was quickly unmasked as false. But for Chinese agriculture the whole debate was enormously harmful. They went as far as to deny the existence of viruses. Some of the orange trees that were known to be affected by viruses could not be treated because the Soviet advisors did not think it would be right. So of course, trees died en masse.[93]

Once Lysenko's critics no longer ran the risk of being branded and punished as fundamental opponents of the USSR, a conference was organized in Qingdao in 1956 on how to deal with Lysenkoism. In only a few hours the Soviet biologist's findings were exposed as absurd and then removed for good from labs and textbooks.

The question of dealing with traditional and modern medicine also returned to the agenda. Early in the 1950s a commission composed primarily of Western-trained physicians was tasked with surveying the diverse theories and practices of Chinese traditional healing and identifying those elements it considered beneficial to a socialist society grounded in the natural sciences. Mao Zedong also felt compelled to enter the debate.[94] In a letter to a member of the General Office of the Central Committee of the CPC in 1958, with the explicit order that his words should be published, he wrote:

The suggestions of the Party members of the Ministry of Health in the final section, i.e. from now on to organize study-classes of 'doctors of Western medicine leaving their profession to study Chinese medicine', should be undertaken by the leading Party members of every province, city and autonomous region. I estimate that if in the year 1958, each province, city and autonomous region sets up one study class of 70–80 'doctors of Western medicine leaving their professions to study Chinese medicine', within the next two years, that is by the winter of 1960 or the spring of 1961, we will have approximately 2,000 of this sort of 'integrating China and the West' high-level medical professionals. Among these, a few brilliant theoretical experts will probably emerge . . .

China's medicine and pharmacy is a great treasure-house, and should be diligently explored and improved upon.[95]

This was the compromise between, on the one hand, immediately abolishing this legacy of the past – a venture that in Mao's opinion would be doomed to fail, since it would deprive countless people of their livelihoods – and on the other, permitting the theory and practice of Chinese medicine to keep existing independently and without restrictions as an alien element in a society otherwise committed to modern science. Mao pointed out the way clearly enough. Western-style doctors had to find and adopt those parts of the treasure-house that were useful. During the Cultural Revolution some ideologues attempted to set other priorities. Pronouncing acupunctural analgesia as dialectically justified, they condemned modern medicine's drug-based anaesthesia as a display of bourgeois metaphysics. Acupuncture, they argued, was effective because it harnessed the inner contradictions of every living thing, while medicinal anaesthesia depended exclusively on outside intervention.[96]

Traditional pharmacy also found support, yet all these ideological attempts at vindication vanished overnight with the end of the leftist-extremist Cultural Revolution. In attitudes toward traditional medicine, the primacy of modern science as it was understood around the world was established once again. Mao Zedong's directive of 1958 to evaluate the ancient practices through the lens of modern medicine and incorporate their useful elements was applied again in full.

Unswervingly and with its objectives always in mind, this policy has continued into the present day. The Chinese government assiduously avoids the impression of disdaining traditional medicine. The leadership takes every opportunity to glorify the great legacy of Chinese healing and its global significance, especially with an eye to its lucrative export possibilities. Meanwhile the country has continued to adopt modern, science-based medicine, step by step. In 2007 the Chinese government invited the ministers of science and healthcare from 50 nations to jointly approve a pre-worded 'Beijing Declaration' that both defines traditional Chinese medicine as 'bio-medicine' while declaring that the future of this medicine lies on molecular biology.

It was also Mao Zedong who initiated or endorsed the various detours that for years would postpone China's return to power, with devastating economic consequences, millions of deaths and traumatized psyches. The most profound breaks were first the Great Leap Forward,[97] which nearly destroyed the national economy and possibly killed tens of millions of people according to reliable estimates, making it one of the most far-reaching crimes against humanity in history,[98] and then the so-called Great Proletarian Cultural Revolution of the latter 1960s, of which the once so articulate Great Chairman never expressed his theory in detail, so that even today his intentions can only be guessed at. The fact is that under the guise of the Cultural Revolution or, perhaps more aptly, in its slipstream, various scores were settled and power struggles fought out, some with incredible brutality. The class struggle, the struggle against the bourgeoisie and feudalism and many other familiar buzzwords of Marxist and Maoist ideology arose here once again, spreading endless suffering throughout the land. Inevitably the quest for a proletarian dictatorship ended in chaos because it proved to be nothing but a destructive illusion.

With the end of the Cultural Revolution and the new course of the People's Republic under the pragmatic policies of Deng Xiaoping, China entered the most recent phase of its recovery from traumatic humiliation. Probably never before has an entire country thrown itself into a campaign to swiftly catch up with other nations in as much detail or with such truly military precision. Innovative economic concepts lured Western hi-tech firms to the beckoning Chinese market. Joint ventures proved especially important by giving Chinese companies access to Western know-how free of charge, thereby helping offset decades of neglect by Chinese companies to quickly develop their own modern technology. The plans to make citizens of the People's Republic world leaders in every scientific, cultural and athletic discipline imaginable are likewise unparalleled in history.[99]

Also truly remarkable is the spectrum of efforts that Mao Zedong demanded in 1940 to push forward the appropriation of all useful aspects of Western culture while keeping attention fixed not only on the present, but also on the past. Today, as in the late nineteenth century, innumerable young people and established scholars have been sent out to the centres of Western science and technology. Creative incentives are forcing Chinese universities to abandon their past lethargy and seek contacts and cooperation with the best academic institutions in the West.

The rewards of this comprehensively planned campaign have been remarkable. The share of the Chinese population still trapped in a premodern, prescientific existence is diminishing rapidly with every new year. Those at the forefront of this trend have helped their country accomplish first-rate feats of technology and, increasingly, of science. After aerospace research was introduced in 1960 using high-performance rockets, China launched its first satellite into orbit in 1970. Two decades later, Chinese technicians again successfully steered the country's first telecommunications satellite into space. A mission to the moon was founded in 2006 with the collaboration of experts at twenty universities; its planned objective was to land a Chinese lunar rover on the moon's surface within eight years: that is, by 2014.

A very recent example of Chinese contributions to global research in quantum teleportation illustrates how much these impressive advances owe to the strenuous efforts of single-mindedly learning from the West. The decision to do so was made a century ago. In 1996 the Chinese sent physicist Pan Jianwei, who had already received the best training at home, to Austria, where he took his doctorate under quantum physicist and Academy of Sciences member Anton Zeilinger, who has gained international renown for his quantum teleportation research. For a while Pan Jianwei moved to Heidelberg. After returning to China in 2008, he directed a research group on quantum communication that in 2011–12 became the first in the world to successfully test the teleportation process over a distance of 100 km using one intermediate station.[100]

One could assemble a long list of other such examples from practically any field of science and technology. As if trying to recover from a deep-seated inferiority complex, China is endeavouring to be 'first' in every cultural aspect possible. In 2003 Chinese authorities were the first to approve marketing of the first commercial gene therapy drug intended for worldwide distribution, Gendicine. The results of scientific and clinical studies legitimating this step were published in Chinese journals in the Chinese language only. Gendicine, the producer claims, is effective in cancer therapy. The Chinese state is an investor in the company producing Gendicine. Under an entirely different system from prevailing international standards, Gendicine received approval prior to completing phase III clinical studies. This provided the producer with a significant advantage over Western researchers and producers working on comparable gene therapies. Their products need first to show their effectiveness in time-consuming phase III studies before they can apply for approval by government authorities.[101]

As for every other country, the Olympic Games have offered China an opportunity to impress the rest of the world with seemingly limitless possibilities for development. For the 2008 Beijing Games the Chinese leadership mobilized all resources to demonstrate to the visitors on the ground and viewers around the world that China had the biggest and most magnificent stadiums and that its people could accomplish the greatest feats of athletic prowess. This determination was again palpable at the 2012 London Games. For several days China led the medals table ahead of the U.S., taking a satisfaction that helps heal its trauma. Occasionally, this obsessive drive for satisfaction takes on tragic dimensions, as when an athlete tearfully apologizes to his compatriots for taking only a silver medal at the Olympic Games. It can also be quite funny, such as when the 2012 Miss World pageant, held in China, crowned – surprise! – a young Chinese woman as its winner.

What matters is that inside China, hardly anyone disapproves of this process. The historical experience of humiliation was a collective one. The determination to never let it happen again is a common goal. Yet the Chinese architects of these policies always kept in mind that measures would be needed to prevent Western technology and science from remaining alien entities in China. Opening Chinese culture and mentality to these imports was and remains an absolute priority.

Hu Shi was one of the first reformers to take a stand against China's (as he saw it) excessively radical disavowal of its own cultural heritage. He pointed at the great psychological strain that taking such a step would inevitably incur: 'How can we Chinese feel at ease in this new world which at first sight appears to be so much at variance with what we have long regarded as our own civilization?'[102] In his doctoral dissertation submitted at Columbia in 1917, titled *The Development of the Logical Method in Ancient China*, he advocated examining many branches of Chinese logical thought, a large number of which for a long time were not even especially well known in China, to arrive at the reassuring appreciation of China's own contribution to the 'New World.'

> It would therefore seem to be the duty of New China to study the long-neglected native systems in the light and with the aid of modern Western philosophy . . . Not until then can [we] truly feel at ease with the new methods and instrumentalities of speculation and research . . . For it is perfectly natural and justifiable that a nation with a glorious past and with a distinctive civilization of its own making should never feel quite at home in a new civilization, if that new civilization is looked upon as part and parcel imported from alien lands and forced upon it by external necessities of national existence. And it would surely be a great loss to mankind at large if the acceptance of this new civilization should take the form of abrupt displacement instead of organic assimilation, thereby causing the disappearance of the old civilization. The real problem, therefore, may be restated thus: How can we best assimilate modern civilization in such a manner as to make it congenial and congruous and continuous with the civilization of our own making?[103]

Hu Shi's call did not go unnoticed. For many decades, it has continued to inform the complex processes of absorbing Western science, logic, mathematics and technology. Spurred by the encounter with Western civilization and alarmed by the dominance of Western culture in practically every segment of daily life, people developed an interest in Chinese history the likes of which had never been seen before. Countless writings by ancient, often

hardly known or indeed long-forgotten authors were rediscov-
ered and re-examined to see how they held up to European
knowledge and achievements. The 'four great discoveries' of the
compass, gunpowder, printing and paper, which, as every Chinese child knows, testify to the early greatness of Chinese culture,
proved especially soothing to the tortured Chinese soul. Ancient
thinkers who stood in even the remotest relationship with modern positions of, say, physics, were declared Chinese 'physicists'.[104]

Some teachings of the ancient philosopher Mo Zi were
accorded the rank of an alternative Chinese logic. The boundless
wealth of Chinese intellectual history was mined as an inex-
haustible source of evidence that the Chinese had long anticipated subsequent European achievements.[105] In texts dating
from the third century BCE Chinese investigators found proof
that telescopes were being built. In one debate over the origi-
nality of Chinese optics, at least one author made the sweeping
declaration that 'all Western processes in optics already existed
in ancient China.'[106]

These writings often reflected isolated ideas that developed
at most a marginal significance in later Chinese history and
therefore played no part in the cumulative progress of science
and technology. However, in no way does this fact reduce their
importance to the interplay of self-doubt and self-affirmation
generated by the confrontation with Western science and technology. Whenever it is pointed out to Chinese nationalists that
Chinese medicine never included surgery, they point, quite
seriously, to the legendary second-century doctor Hua Tuo, who
allegedly performed operations with anesthetic. Actually, this
Hua Tuo – if he ever really existed – founded no tradition in
surgery, stands as a solitary figure in ancient Chinese medicine
and cannot in the least be compared to the ranks of real people
who helped advance the practice of surgery in Europe. Similarly,
Chinese popular science media do not shrink from portraying
the development of the atomic bomb as an organic continuation
of the Chinese discovery of gunpowder.[107]

As early as in the 1920s, broad-based and forward-looking
steps that heeded the warnings of Hu Shi were taken to eliminate

the possibility that the broader population could develop aversions toward Western achievements. One example was a weekly periodical that always included an article that, at first glance from a Western perspective, is easily belittled. Each of these articles was dedicated to a different Western technological advance, such as the telegraph, the x-ray machine and the airplane. The article covering the x-ray machine, for example, included a drawn illustration of the machine in medical use. The author quoted a 2,000-year-old classic text that, in this context, implied that ideas of peering through an individual to recognize his innermost workings already existed in ancient China. Then came a modern commentary saying, in effect: 'Look! This is actually an ancient facet of Chinese culture. We never believed it was necessary to develop it further. Now the West has produced this technology from it. We should remind ourselves of our ancient, pioneering achievements and join in current developments.' Finding examples like this for the telegraph or aeroplane and many other inventions in ancient texts was fairly easy. One could always find a case of someone saying something somewhere and being heard far away – or even more simply, someone arriving somewhere by flying. The implicit purpose of these articles was to prevent foreign inventions from giving rise to any sense of cultural inferiority among the Chinese, who might then proceed to reject the inventions of foreign cultures in a wholesale manner.

When the Communist Party took power in 1949, all references in the press to real or alleged 'China first' achievements were banned. To the internationalist-minded party ideologues, the threat of nationalist arrogance seemed to outweigh the psychological boost of feeling not so inferior to the West after all.[108] When China again 'opened up' in the 1970s, ways were again found internally to raise awareness of modern science among those parts of the population unable to study abroad or otherwise make contact with the modern world.

However, one cannot overlook the ongoing efforts of more than a handful of Chinese authors to demonstrate that many traditions have a legitimate right to survive in the modern world, much as traditional Chinese medicine does. For example, TCM also stands for traditional Chinese mathematics, and no less an intellectual luminary than Wu Wenjun (*b.* 1919) regards Chinese mathematics as more than a source of ideas for modern mathematics. In his writings he also says that there are very good reasons for the continued existence of mathematics that are autonomous, effective and founded exclusively on Chinese approaches.[109]

Television documentaries and historical films about scientific episodes in Europe reach large audiences in cities and rural areas. The national leadership uses these media both to add historical facts and events to the people's general education and subtly introduce certain manners of cultural behaviour to the Chinese mentality. For example, on Chinese television one can find convincingly produced films about a late medieval European monk who irritates those around him, and especially his superiors, with new ideas. Refusing to abandon them despite constant pressure and resistance, he finally matures his ideas and puts them to use – for the benefit of all civilization.

This is also the context in which the exhibition 'The Art of the Enlightenment' should be seen. After opening, together with the biggest museum in the world, in Beijing on 1 April 2011, the show gave the Chinese public an opportunity for a whole year to think about the intellectual revolution that launched Europe's breakout from its 'self-incurred immaturity'. The Chinese term for enlightenement is *qi meng*. It is not an artificial neologism that first has to be given meaning, like *ke xue* for 'science'. This term, which basically means 'bringing knowledge to an unknowing child', has been in continuous circulation for 2,000 years and is often used metaphorically to denote the overcoming of prejudice and ignorance.

Liu Xianting (1648–1695), a Chinese scholar who criticized his peers for their excessive preoccupation with the past and considered himself dedicated to scientific advancement, once wrote:

Oh woe! How deep in the dark the inner laws of things lie; how superficial man's knowledge is. If only countless knowing men could come forth in the world to liberate me and eliminate the obstacles [on the path to understanding].

For every Chinese person who has gone to school, the term *qi meng* raises associations closely related to the European understanding of 'enlightenment'. In addition, many books concerning the causes and effects of the European Enlightenment have for decades been available in Chinese. The exhibition was a further sign of the Chinese leadership's intent to acquaint the population with European events. One question this raises for us is whether we should care to concern ourselves as intensively with Chinese culture as China is concerned with the intellectual history of Europe.

The opening of the Beijing show, stocked by Germany's three big state museums in Berlin, Dresden and Munich and financed by carmaker BMW, met with almost unanimous disapproval in the German press. This was attributable in part to the imprisonment some time ago of regime critic Liu Xiaobo and other, less prominent writers who stood up to the Communist regime. However, just before the exhibition's opening it was the detention of Ai Weiwei, a greatly popular artist in the West, which prompted journalists to question the show's entire premise.

Critics' fears that the exhibition was pointless because the Chinese leadership ignored principles that the Enlightenment inspired in Europe are based on a fundamental misunderstanding. Knowing it has the support of most of the population, and not least out of respect to its own culture, the Chinese government has no interest in joining the greater circle of Western civilization. Obviously, however, the lifestyle and freedoms taken for granted in the West are also highly attractive in China and gladly accepted by many people. The term for enlightenment, *qi meng*, has positive connotations in Chinese and, in conjunction with a visually striking exhibition of European art, meets a receptive public.

The important thing is to constantly remain aware of China's size and the heterogeneity of its people. Just as the idea of 'science' was and remains a conceptually alien body in Chinese culture, for more than a few Chinese the idea of 'Enlightenment', as Europeans understand it, is likewise alien. In a reflex-like protective response, these people consider the Enlightenment's call for political liberty quite aggravating. The author Gan Yang, dean of Sun Yat-Sen University's Institute for Advanced Studies in Humanities, used an event accompanying the 'Art and Enlightenment' exhibition in autumn 2011 to publicly voice his disdain for the philosopher Immanuel Kant and his quite restrictive view of the goals of the European Enlightenment. He reduced these to the liberation from a superstition that held sway during a particular period in history. Gan Yang concluded his remarks with the following 'personal' analysis:

> If we ask what kind of enlightenment China needs today, must we not ask first, what is the biggest superstition of modern China? The way I see it, the answer is clear: The biggest superstition of today's China is in the superstition toward the West and in particular toward the Second Western Enlightenment. It is precisely this modern superstition in China today that causes virtually no one to use his 'own mind' to question it, because all are of the opinion that they require the 'mind of the people of the West'. Likewise, Chinese thinkers and public opinion in China cannot, at least currently, get by 'without the instructions of others', since they think they cannot exist without the 'instructions of the Westerners'.[110]

Gan Yang certainly did not reflect the general political line of the Chinese government, which was and remains aware of Chen Duxiu's 'Solemn Appeal to the Youth' from 1915. The fact that some of Gan's listeners applauded enthusiastically is further evidence that the trauma of having to adapt to the West in order to stand up to it has in no way healed. Others in the young audience found the attempt to distance China from the West rather amusing.

The Chinese public does not just exist in China behind a Great Wall, watched closely by the Communist Party. Countless Chinese people now also live in the U.S. and Europe, feel quite happy there and have first-hand experience of the benefits and drawbacks of Western culture. These people do not build ghetto-like societies that close themselves off from Western values. They have no problem adapting to Western living and finding their places as scientists in Western research institutions. Most significantly, however, most of these expatriate Chinese remain in close contact with relatives and friends back home. Influences such as this give Chinese society a momentum that not even the government can stop, regardless of how restrictive its policies may be.

Recent initiatives by Chinese reformist educators are an example. There are no known initiatives within Chinese government circles to reform the country's education system, which was established more than half a century ago for a socialist society and command economy, to meet the new demands of the global market. Currently, pupils engage in mechanistic rote learning of some basic knowledge and certain basic abilities that appeared necessary when the People's Republic was in its infancy. Reformers, including Jiang Xueqin, who have returned to China from the United States and other Western countries, are calling on the authorities to fashion an educational system that encourages Chinese pupils to be creative and imaginative and to analyse problems critically. The reformers hope that in this way the country can produce more world-class scientists, overcoming a deficit that is often considered embarrassing. These kinds of initiatives by returning émigrés are clear evidence that China's future will be influenced from many sides and an increasingly heterogeneous population. Even if some voices lament the loss of the 'Chinese essence' in this cultural evolution, the decisive factor will be the opinion of the majority, which regards Western culture as a quarry from which China must take the construction materials needed for a successful future.[111]

From the humiliations of the nineteenth and twentieth centuries and an assortment of episodes of Western policies towards countries of the developing world in recent decades, China has learned that it can depend only on itself to muster the strength necessary to defend its interests, if necessary against those of the West. From the Chinese perspective, the values the West invokes in judging Chinese actions, especially in domestic policy, are just empty phrases. Beijing knows from its own extensive experience the actions with which the West not infrequently discredits these values.

It was an irony of history that, just as prominent individuals in Germany and other Western countries were protesting against the arrest of Ai Weiwei with signature-gathering campaigns and other initiatives, confidential documents regarding presumably innocent people being held by the United States in Guantánamo Bay were made public. The coincidence again showed the existence of a highly problematic system of double standards, and not only from the Chinese perspective.

An unbiased comparison of how human rights are upheld by the policies of Western states on the one hand and the situation in China on the other would hardly result in the stark, black-and-white contrast that many people in the West claim to see. Guantánamo is a response to the trauma of 9/11 that many outsiders consider harsh but U.S. authorities regard as completely legitimate. The 'war on terror', with its many victims on both sides, is supposed to prevent another humiliation of the U.S. on the scale of 9/11. Similarly, the traumas inflicted on China in the nineteenth and early twentieth centuries prompt the current leadership there to take certain steps against individuals who appear to threaten the current state. From the outside these steps appear excessive, yet the leadership considers the steps justified.

Over and over, Western observers have lamented the 'disproportionate severity' with which Chinese authorities act against critics of the regime. This is another instance of ignorance of Chinese crisis management. In the second century BCE the philosopher Xunzi announced: 'the gentleman intervenes to ensure order where order still exists. He does not attempt to ensure order when disorder already reigns.' This is also a core approach in Chinese medical theory and is therefore deeply rooted in Chinese collective consciousness. At the slightest sign of approaching illness, intervention takes place immediately. The idea of waiting in the face of approaching crisis is alien to Chinese thinking, both in medicine and politics. This, however, is precisely the scenario that the Chinese government sees. Disorder is everywhere. Western military interventions can be found wherever change in a direction agreeable to the West cannot come fast enough. The Chinese government takes no risks and removes its critics from visibility, sometimes ruthlessly, before their small numbers can multiply into a mass movement.

If collective reason in China has managed to push through acceptance of science, logic and many other characteristics of Western thinking, it is primarily because Chinese traditional knowledge – that is, the relationist doctrines of Yin-Yang and the Five Phases of Change – cannot make light bulbs glow or mobile phones ring, nor launch a rocket so much as a millimetre off the ground. China wants power. Regaining power means knowing one's rival intimately, including his cultural and intellectual foundations – in this case the Enlightenment. The fact that the exhibition's originators also financed this acquaintance to the tune of €10 million is, for the Chinese, both a pleasing accompaniment and a masterpiece of their cultural diplomacy.

Besides errors in judging the motivations of the Chinese authorities, another reason for the uneasiness, especially in the German media, towards the exhibition in question may have been regret that a non-Western nation led by an authoritarian Communist Party could be in a position to go its own way, causing substantial problems for Western economies while ensuring big profits for German industry with its hunger for consumer and investment goods. Today the Chinese government is in a position to simultaneously hold power, ensure domestic stability and expand China's importance and influence internationally while ignoring those who condemn as unacceptable the steps it takes to achieve these goals.

The traumas inflicted upon China in the nineteenth and early twentieth centuries were deep-seated and had lasting repercussions that conditioned both the country's domestic and foreign policies. One example is policy toward religion. China has a freedom of religion that exists in hardly any other country. Yet the government refuses to grant the people freedom of association. That means that an individual's or group's choice of religion is utterly unimportant, both to the government and these people's peers. Yet distrust of, for example, Christians who submit to a foreign organization, as Catholics do to the Vatican, is deep-seated because of historical experiences with the political activities of Christian missionaries, so China denies the devout the right to associate, though not their freedom of religion. When Western policy-makers demand freedom of association under the umbrella of religious freedom, they simply bolster that mistrust, for the two freedoms are not synonymous.[112]

For Western policy, the decisive consideration should be the fact that China bases its power interests on a scientific and cultural foundation that European science and culture at least does not dispute. No one, least of all the Chinese leadership, would deny the substantial differences that exist between China and Western societies in guaranteeing certain rights of the individual. Anyone feeling him- or herself able to solve this problem quickly need only lift a finger and suggest appropriate, thoughtful solutions that go beyond simplified declamations. The leaders in China will listen gladly, but they know the conditions in their country and how difficult it is to lead a population from one cultural context to a completely different one relatively peacefully, and the pitfalls that await when the steps into the future are not carefully considered. Judging events in China from the outside and without responsibility is certainly simpler than having to make the necessary decisions every day.

When observing Chinese politics, one must distinguish between two realities in the country. The first is the current political structure, which in many ways is marked by the will of the leadership to cement its power in a way that runs athwart of Western ideas of democracy, and which is therefore regularly and sharply condemned. How to deal with these incompatibilities and whether this reality will see real change over the medium term are matters for day-to-day politics. For the West's fundamental stance toward China, a stance that must outlast day-to-day politics, it is the second reality of China, that of its old cultural characteristics, that is important. These characteristics suggest that, despite all today's rivalries, a sensible partnership can grow between us.

Conclusion

REGARDLESS OF THE success of its efforts to pull even with the West in terms of technology and to amass huge amounts of foreign currency reserves, China is still not a wealthy country when seen in its entirety. While most people no longer must fear starvation, living conditions among broad segments of both the urban and rural population remain very modest and are sometimes marked by poverty. The revolution of the late 1940s and the campaigns of the following years resulted in the expropriation of magnates and eliminated 'capitalists' in the cities as well. For a while it seemed that all starry-eyed fans of extreme leftist policy could look to China as the New Man took the political stage there, after the Soviet model generated only limited enthusiasm in the West. For several years now, however, the wealthy have returned to China and the high-handed manner of many local officials has been reminiscent of the imperious bureaucracy of old.

Anyone visiting China today in search of signs of a 'socialist' mentality or policy will find them only in the rhetoric of the Communist Party, if at all. The Party reserves the leading role for itself and continues to be based on Marxism, albeit the pragmatic version modified by Deng Xiaoping. The country still cannot afford a comprehensive social welfare system. That is due on the one hand to the economic restrictions that still exist and on the other – and perhaps more importantly – because the rhetoric obviously has so little in common with the country's cultural traditions. In the several decades it has been available, no amount of Marxist or socialist sloganeering has managed to achieve much of note in China.

The expectation that China would acquire a social or even socialist mentality by founding a People's Republic under Marxist-

Leninist principles, headed by a Communist Party, was just as naive and the demand much the same as the idea that China's collective culture could produce a parliamentary, multi-party democracy. The necessary fundamental trust, which in Europe took centuries and many bloody wars to slowly evolve, does not exist in China. A pervasive mistrust of all people not bound by family, a teacher-pupil relationship or associations dedicated to a cause, together with a traditional winner-takes-all attitude toward losers, are all obstacles that cannot be removed from one day to the next or even in the foreseeable future.

Parliamentary democracy is based on the trust that, having won an election, a leader will not solely promote the interests of his or her electoral clientele. The victor pledges to protect the greater community and respects political rivals' right to exist. Comparable demands were made in ancient Confucianism, but they failed to find a response in Chinese culture. In most European societies, trust in a rival's good will and respect for his right to exist still constitute the foundation of parliamentary democracy.

It is unknown whether China's present political reality is capable of developing a higher degree of social policy or even European structures. The more likely direction would be towards conditions in the United States.

Certainly, one great difference between the u.s. and China will remain in place for a long time to come: at least parts of America's population still live the ideals of Europe's social traditions, whether in Sunday sermons calling on others to be charitable or in secular organizations such as the American Civil Liberties Union, which fights for the human rights of all citizens, regardless of their politics, background or personal life. Still, the differences with Europe, where the transition to culturally heterogeneous societies is still taking place, with painful consequences for many, are unmistakable.

In Germany, for example, every worker is forced to deduct substantial sums from his or her pay, for example, for health and retirement insurance, without knowing who benefits from this. These residual structures of societies in solidarity are taken for granted by most Europeans. In the U.S. a politically influential segment of the populace considers these structures to be spawns of communism that interfere with one's own responsibility. Indeed, conservatives wield one of the most effective rhetorical weapons in America today when they say that the President's policies are 'European'. Therefore when a U.S. judge in Florida struck down President Obama's mandatory healthcare law in January 2011, he explicitly stated that the law requiring citizens to buy health insurance or pay a fine 'imperils individual liberty'. This is the sound of American cultural heterogeneity, in which solidarity that spans various groups – except in times of external danger – is an alien idea to many Americans. People observing the United States from a Chinese perspective understand this better than Europeans do.

For the Chinese person wanting to leave his or her homeland, these parallels, together with higher living standards and greater individual freedoms, are not the only reasons why America is far more attractive than Europe. In the personal struggle to secure one's existence, the individual in China and the U.S. depends largely on him- or herself and must try to make the best of the possibilities at hand.

Europe and China are neighbours via Russia. In the conflicts of the past two centuries, none of those involved can claim to be free of all culpability. Colonialism, exploitation and repression were facets of policy on all sides – whether toward one's geographical neighbours or on the other side of the world. It is very hard to tell whether the future will be free of such problematic political approaches, despite all the new international organizations and other structural links.

The most important consideration in European policy towards China should be the common sense with which China is adapting its culture to the demands of the future. This common sense – which the preceding discussion and analysis has sought to suggest – offers the great opportunity of a giant cultural space stretching from Western Europe to Beijing and Shanghai. This megaspace could stand out from other regions where external control of existence by numinous powers is again taking an increasingly central cultural position.

One observes the growing threat of serious scientific training in American schools being endangered by the efforts of religious fundamentalists and the economic interests of those who see their business interests harmed by scientifically founded signs of looming, catastrophic climate change. In this light, China, with its strict reliance on secular, modern natural science and technology, could soon gain the advantage over the u.s. and prove more compatible with the secular European world-view.

China and Europe could meet in their efforts to provide people with the existential self-determination for which the sciences strive. In both the western and eastern regions of the great Eurasian continent, rich traditions of secular values exist that, if the necessary good will is also present, could enable people to live together more peacefully than they could in the past.

A cursory glance at the Chinese policy of adopting the Western natural and social sciences might lead one to conclude that the Chinese variant of dealing with the once-so-menacing civilization of the West does not constitute a 'clash of cultures'. Doing so would not do justice to the facts, however. What we have examined here has been rather a very subtle clash of cultures. 'My fate lies in my hands, not in those of heaven' – these words to live by were, together with the greatest tactical finesse, the foundation for China's re-emergence.

The West appears to have forgotten this attitude. In Germany and elsewhere, political parties, whose voters are ready to take responsibility for their lives and depend on their own initiative to make a living, have been reduced to minority status. The essential balance between individual and social responsibility has been lost. The individual's demands on 'society' are rising in all areas and long ago overloaded the system's capacity to support them. The efforts of some government to set policies requiring more individual responsibility from people under pressure from rising debt generally encounter incomprehension and culminate either in the advocates of such policies being voted out of office or enraged protest on the streets.

With poverty and indebtedness on the rise as industries migrate to China, and as China's export prowess only grows, the West is not taking the path that China opted for. Instead of analysing its own deficiencies, it blames China for its woes. In the same manner that some European leaders seek to reduce Germany's economic dominance by insisting that Germany slash its productivity, Western politicians have demanded in response to China's economic resurgence that the Chinese change their ways, including letting their currency appreciate. The mentality of seeking responsibility for one's own problems among those one blames for the problems is affecting Europe. For the West, despite successes in science and technology, 'my fate lies in my hands' is no longer a guiding principle. In any case, the West is for now incapable of devising its own, innovative models for the future that could demonstrate China's own limitations.

Pointing that out was left to Chinese premier Wen Jiabao, during the German chancellor Angela Merkel's visit on 2 February 2012. As Wen reminded the Europeans, 'the key to overcoming the debt crisis must be Europe's own effort.'

References

1 The following account of individual episodes is based on
   data that can be read in detail in many works: Brunhild
   Staiger, Stefan Friedrich and Hans-Wilm Schütte, eds, *Das
   grosse China Lexikon* (Darmstadt, 2008); John K. Fairbank,
   ed., *The Cambridge History of China*, vol. XII: *Republican
   China, 1912–1949* (Cambridge, 1983); Jonathan Spence,
   The Search for Modern China (New York and London,
   1990); Conrad Schirokauer, *A Brief History of Chinese and
   Japanese Civilizations* (San Diego and New York, 1978);
   Helwig Schmidt-Glintzer, *Kleine Geschichte Chinas*
   (Munich, 2008); Franz-Josef Kemnade, 'Opiumkriege
   und Taiping-Aufstand, Entstehung des aussenpolitischen
   Konflikts und seine Beziehungen zur innenpolitischen
   Krise', GRIN Verlag für akademische Texte, no. V89778
   (2010), and other standard works on Chinese history.
2 In E. Backhouse and J.O.P. Bland, *Annals and Memoirs of
   the Court of Peking* (Boston, MA, 1914), pp. 322–31.
3 Fairbank, ed., *The Cambridge History of China*, vol. X: *Late
   Ch'ing, 1800–1911, Part 1* (Cambridge, 1978), pp. 175–6.
4 In the document, the characters in the Chinese translitera-
   tion of the name 'Napier' were selected so as to read
   'strained despicable beast'.
5 Priscilla H. Napier, *Barbarian Eye: Lord Napier in China,
   1834. The Prelude to Hong Kong* (London, 1995), pp. 167–8.
   See also William Caraway, 'A Clash of Cultures', chap. 17
   of 'Korea in the Eye of the Tiger', at
   www.koreanhistoryproject.org, accessed 19 November 2012.
6 Napier, *Barbarian Eye*, p. 147.
7 See also Schmidt-Glintzer, *Kleine Geschichte Chinas*, p. 117.
8 See also Spence, *The Search for Modern China*.
9 Ssu-yu Teng and John K. Fairbank, *China's Response to the
   West* (Cambridge, MA, 1954), pp. 24–7.

10 In the calculation of the time, 6 million taels, of which
    4 million went to the British and 2 million to the French.

11 'This little dog was found by me in the Palace of Yuan-
    Ming-Yuan near Pekin on 6 October 1860. It is supposed to
    have belonged to either the Empress or one of the ladies of
    the Imperial Family. It is a most affectionate and intelligent
    little creature - it has always been accustomed to be treated
    as a pet and it was with the hope that it might be looked
    upon as such by Her Majesty and the Royal Family that I
    have brought it from China.' J. Hart Dunne, K. Captain 99th
    Regt, quoted on 'Pekingese', www.champdogs.co.uk,
    accessed 19 November 2012.

12 Anon., *Der Krieg gegen China im Jahre 1860* (Leipzig, 1865),
    p. 106.

13 Joseph Buttinger, *The Smaller Dragon: A Political History of
    Vietnam* (New York 1958).

14 Charles D. Benn, *Daily Life in Traditional China: The Tang
    Dynasty* (Santa Barbara, CA, 2002), p. 28.

15 For subsequent details, see Frédéric Mantienne, *Mon-
    seigneur Pigneau de Béhaine* (Paris, 1999), and James P.
    Daughton, 'Recasting Pigneau de Behaine: Missionaries and
    the Politics of French Colonial History, 1884–1914', in *Viet
    Nam Borderless Histories*, ed. Nhung Tuyet Tran and
    Anthony J. S. Reid (Ann Arbor, MI, 2006), pp. 290–322.

16 'Die Aussenpolitik der USA und der Sowjetunion angesichts
    der japanischen und deutschen Expansion bis 1941', at
    www.zum.de, accessed 19 November 2012.

17 Chunxiao Jing, *Mit Barbaren gegen Barbaren. Die
    chinesische Selbststärkungsbewegung und das deutsche
    Rüstungsgeschäft im späten 19. Jahrhundert* (Berlin, Zürich
    and Münster, 2002), pp. 60ff.

18 Cord Eberspächer, *Die deutsche Yangtse-Patrouille.
    Deutsche Kanonenbootpolitik in China im Zeitalter des
    Imperialismus 1900–1914*. Kleine Schriftenreihe zur
    Militär- und Marinegeschichte, vol. VIII (Bochum, 2004).

19 Report by Paul Jaeschke on the expedition to Ichowfu
    Prefecture, Tsingtau, 29 March 1899, Politisches Archiv des
    Auswärtigen Amtes, Bonn (PA), China 22: Kiautschou-
    Schantung, vol. IV.

20 See also Mechthild Leutner and Klaus Mühlhahn, eds,
    Deutsch-chinesische Beziehungen im 19. Jahrhundert:

Mission und Wirtschaft in interkultureller Perspektive
(Münster, 2001).

21 On the Empress Dowager Cixi and the grotesque distortions of her life in Western literature, see Sterling Seagrave, *Dragon Lady: The Life and Legend of the Last Empress of China* (New York, 1993).

22 Ralph Erbar, '*Kein Pardon! Die 'Hunnenrede' Wilhelms II. und ihre Geschichte*', in *Politische Reden. Deutschland im 20. Jahrhundert* (Braunschweig, 2007), pp. 14–17; Johannes Penzler, ed., *Die Reden Kaiser Wilhelms II*, vol. II: *1896–1900* (Leipzig, n.d.), pp. 209–12. Manfred Görtemaker: *Deutschland im 19. Jahrhundert. Entwicklungslinien*, Schriftenreihe der Bundeszentrale für politische Bildung, Bd. 274 (Opladen, 1996), p. 357.

23 See also Mechthild Leutner and Klaus Mühlhahn, eds, *Kolonialkrieg in China. Die Niederschlagung der Boxerbewegung, 1900–1901* (Berlin, 2007).

24 Fairbank, ed., *The Cambridge History of China*, vol. XII, Part 1, pp. 177–82.

25 Reliable studies estimate that Japan's acts of warfare and occupation in East and Southeast Asia between 1931 and 1945 caused more than 17 million deaths. In one pointless orgy of violence, for example, the Japanese army alone killed more Philippine civilians in Manila after U.S. troops landed in the Philippines than there were Japanese civilians killed by the blast of the atomic bomb dropped on Nagasaki. The Japanese army and civilians also used unfathomably cruel methods to kill one-third of all Allied prisoners of war during the Second World War. See Richard B. Frank, *Downfall: The End of the Imperial Japanese Empire* (New York, 1999), pp. 26; 160–63.

26 Ibid., pp. 324–6. See also Jing Bao Nie et al., ed., *Japanese Wartime Medical Atrocities: Comparative Inquiries in Science, History, and Ethics* (London, 2010).

27 Erwin Wickert, ed., *John Rabe. Der gute Deutsche von Nanking* (Stuttgart, 1997); Kenneth Scott Latourette, *The Chinese: Their History and Culture* (New York, 1967), p. 351: 'scenes of wholesale rape and the slaughter of helpless prisoners and civilians, which shocked the civilized world.'

28 For an acccount at least partially driven by the emotions of

a Chinese-American author, see Iris Chang, *The Rape of Nanking: The Forgotten Holocaust of World War II* (New York, 2012). For an attempt by a Japanese author to relativize the dimensions of Japanese atrocities, see Takashi Yoshida, *The Making of the 'Rape of Nanking': History and Memory in Japan, China, and the United States*, Studies of the Weatherhead East Asian Institute, Columbia University (New York, 2009).

29 See Bernard Lewis, *What Went Wrong? The Clash between Islam and Modernity in the Middle East* (New York, 2003).

30 Andrian Kreye, 'Die Wurzeln des Bösen. Ekel und Hass prägten die islamistischen Grundsatztexte des ägyptischen Literaturwissenschaftlers Sayyid Qutb', *Süddeutsche Zeitung*, no. 102, 4 May 2011, p. 11. See also media reports on anti-German incidents ('Deutschenhass') in German schoolyards with high percentages of children with migrant backgrounds. Those youths involved have been exclusively from culturally Islamic families, and none whose parents had come from China, Korea, Japan or Vietnam.

31 Michel Strickmann, *Chinese Magical Medicine*, ed. Bernard Faure (Stanford, CA, 2002).

32 *Mencius*, Book 4, chapter 1, para. 13.

33 *Lunyu*, Book 12, chapter 6, para. 4.

34 Paul A. Cohen, *Speaking to History: The Story of King Goujian in Twentieth-century China* (Berkeley and Los Angeles, 2010).

35 Harro von Senger, *Moulüe - Supraplanung: Unerkannte Denkhorizonte aus dem Reich der Mitte* (Munich, 2008).

36 *Lunyu*, Book 12, ch. 6, para. 3.

37 Strickmann, *Chinese Magical Medicine*, pp. 1ff.

38 *Suwen*, chapter 3. Paul U. Unschuld and Hermann Tessenow, *Huang Di Nei Jing Su Wen: Annotated Translation* (Berkeley and Los Angeles, 2011), vol. I, p. 81.

39 *Suwen*, chapter 74; Unschuld and Tessenow, *Huang Di Nei Jing Su Wen*, vol. II, p. 642.

40 *Suwen*, chapter 25; Unschuld and Tessenow, *Huang Di Nei Jing Su Wen*, vol. II, p. 419.

41 Chinese. *Wo ming zai wo, bu zai tian* 我命在我不在天.

42 Karl-Heinz Kohl, *Die Macht der Dinge. Geschichte und Theorie sakraler Objekte* (Munich, 2003), p. 86.

43 Chinese: *shang xia tong fa* 上下同法.

44 Johann Peter Frank, *System einer vollständigen medizinis-*
    chen Polizey, vols I–IV (Mannheim, 1779).

45 Heinrich Schipperges, *Moderne Medizin im Spiegel der*
    Geschichte (Stuttgart, 1970), p. 104: 'Die Überlieferung der
    ‚sex res non naturales' bezog sich auf folgende Punkte: 1.
    Aer – Licht und Luft, 2. Cibus et Potus – Speis und Trank.
    3. Motus et Quies – Arbeit und Ruhe. 4. Somnus et Vigilia –
    Schlafen und Wachen. 5. Excreta et Secreta – Ausscheidun-
    gen und Absonderungen. 6 Affectus Animi – Leiden-
    schaften.'

46 See also Benjamin A. Elman, *On Their Own Terms: Science*
    in China, 1550–1900 (Cambridge, MA, and London, 2005).

47 Despite all of this pioneering work's forgivable errors and
    misjudgments, the multi-volume work by British natural
    scientist and scientific historian Joseph Needham and his
    staff and colleagues remains the most impressive document
    of Chinese achievements in the understanding of nature
    and technology of the past two millennia and more: *Science*
    and Civilisation in China (Cambridge, 1958–2008).

48 Richard Wilhelm, *Li Gi. Das Buch der Sitte des Älteren und*
    Jüngeren Dai. Aufzeichnungen über Kultur und Religion des
    alten China (Jena, 1930), pp. 21–2. 格物、致知、诚意、正
    心、修身、齐家、治国、平天下.

49 Paul U. Unschuld, *Medicine in China: A History of Ideas*
    (Berkeley and Los Angeles, CA, 2010), pp. 106–07.

50 Chunxiao Jing, *Mit Barbaren gegen Barbaren*, p. 33.

51 Ibid., pp. 15ff.

52 Spence, *The Search for Modern China*.

53 Ibid.

54 D.W.Y. Kwok, *Scientism in Chinese Thought, 1900–1950*
    (New Haven, CT, and London, 1965), p. 5.

55 Chunxiao Jing, *Mit Barbaren gegen Barbaren*, pp. 15ff.

56 Ibid., p. 28.

57 Kwok, *Scientism in Chinese Thought*, p. 4.

58 Tsien Tsuen-hsuin, 'Western Impact on China Through
    Translation', *Far Eastern Quarterly*, XIII/3 (May 1954),
    p. 317.

59 Chunxiao Jing, *Mit Barbaren gegen Barbaren*, p. 46.

60 Kwok, *Scientism in Chinese Thought*, p. 6.

61 Yan Fu, *Mu le ming xue* 穆勒名學 ('Mill's Logic'), quoted in
    Joachim Kurtz, 'De-modernizing Chinese Logic', lecture

given on 25 July 2011 at the 13th International Conference on the History of Science in East Asia, in Hefei/Anhui, P.R. of China.

62 David Wright, 'Yan Fu and the Tasks of the Translator', in *New Terms for New Ideas: Western Knowledge and Lexical Change in Late Imperial China*, ed. Michael Lackner, Iwo Amelung and Joachim Kurtz (Leiden, 2001), pp. 235–56.

63 Schirokauer, *A Brief History of Chinese and Japanese Civilizations*, pp. 476ff.

64 Kwok, *Scientism in Chinese Thought*, p. 12.

65 Ibid., p. 11.

66 Paul U. Unschuld, *What is Medicine? Western and Eastern Approaches to Healing* (Berkeley and Los Angeles, CA, 2009).

67 Paul U. Unschuld, *Medicine in China: Historical Artefacts and Images* (Munich, London and New York, 2000), pp. 108–09.

68 Xu Dachun, *Yixue yuanliu lun*, translated into English in Paul U. Unschuld, *Forgotten Traditions of Ancient Chinese Medicine* (Brookline, MA, 1998).

69 Unschuld, *Medicine in China*, pp. 212–13.

70 Wu Lien-Te, *Plague Fighter: The Autobiography of a Modern Chinese Physician* (Cambridge, 1959).

71 Wu Yu-lin, *Memories of Dr Wu Lien-Teh: Plague Fighter* (Singapore, 1995), pp. 64 and 100.

72 Ralph C. Croizier, *Traditional Medicine in Modern China* (Cambridge, MA, 1968), pp. 73.

73 Edward V. Gulick, *Peter Parker and the Opening of China* (Cambridge, MA, 1974); Louis Kervyn, *Methode de l'apostolat moderne en Chine* (Hong Kong, 1911), quoted in Kenneth Scott Latourette, *A History of Christian Missions in China* (New York, 1967), p. 561.

74 Gulick, *Peter Parker and the Opening of China*, pp. 20 and 132f.

75 Harold Balme, *China and Modern Medicine* (London, 1921), pp. 104–05.

76 Benjamin A. Elman, 'Rethinking the Twentieth Century Denigration of Traditional Chinese Science and Medicine in the Twenty-first Century', paper prepared for the 6th International Conference on The New Significance of Chinese Culture in the Twenty-first Century: 'The Interaction and

Confluence of Chinese and Non-Chinese Civilization',
co-sponsored by the Himalaya Foundation and the Chiang
Ching-kuo Foundation, and held at the International
Sinological Center at Charles University in Prague, Czech
Republic, 1–2 November 2003.

77 Charlotte Furth, *Ting Wen-chiang: Science and China's New
Culture* (Cambridge, MA, 1970).

78 Kwok, *Scientism in Chinese Thought*, p. 143, cited from Ding
Wenjiang, Xuanxue yu kexue – ping Zhang Junmai de
'renshengguan' (Metaphysics and Science. A Critique of
Zhang Junmai's 'View of Life'). See also Fairbank, ed., *The
Cambridge History of China*, vol. X, 1983, p. 440.

79 Guy Alitto: *The Last Confucian: Liang Shu-Ming and the
Chinese Dilemma of Modernity* (Berkeley and Los Angeles,
CA, 1979).

80 Guorong Yang, 'The Debate Between Scienticists and
Metaphysicians in Early Twentieth Century: Its Theme and
Significance', *Dao: A Journal of Comparative Philosophy*,
II/1 (2002), pp. 79–95.

81 Kwok, *Scientism in Chinese Thought*, p. 141.

82 Ibid., pp. 140ff; Schirokauer, *A Brief History of Chinese and
Japanese Civilizations*, pp. 478–9.

83 Kwok, *Scientism in Chinese Thought*, p. 146.

84 Ibid., pp. 159–60.

85 Iwo Amelung, 'Shaping the Picture of "Chinese Optics":
The Reception of Western Knowledge and the Formation
of Research into a Field of Indigenous Science', lecture given
on 26 July 2011 at the 13th International Conference on the
History of Science in East Asia, in Hefei/Anhui, P.R. of
China.

86 See also Paul U. Unschuld, *Ware Gesundheit. Das Ende der
klassischen Medizin* (Munich, 2009), pp. 35ff.

87 See also the remarks of the poet Liao Yiwu in an interview
with the *Berliner Zeitung* on 16 July 2011 reflecting on his
years in a Chinese prison: 'Reading Elie Wiesel I noticed
how different the Jews and the Chinese are. The Jews have a
collective spirit. Faced with the crematoriums, they sang together. They sang a song that sounded like, "The world is a
narrow bridge that we have to walk over. We cannot stay on
it." Among the Chinese there is no solidarity. They all die
alone. Each is individually tortured and abused. Each one

experiences this as his own, and solely as his own, destiny.'
Arno Widmann, 'Ich bin das Tonbandgerät meiner Epoche',
at www.berlinonline.de, accessed 18 July 2011.

88   Schmidt-Glintzer, *Kleine Geschichte Chinas*, p. 194.

89   Laurence Schneider, *Biology and Revolution in Twentieth-
     century China* (Lanham, MD, 2003), p. 3.

90   'x. Die Alten und die neuen drei Volksprinzipien', at
     www.infopartisan.net/archive/maowerke; 'On New Democ-
     racy', www.marxists.org, both accessed 19 November 2012

91   Schneider, *Biology and Revolution in Twentieth-century
     China*, pp. 2–5.

92   Ibid., p. 9.

93   Ulrike Unschuld, *Wilhelm Mann. Eine Biographie*,
     unpublished manuscript, pers. comm.

94   Kim Taylor, *Chinese Medicine in Early Communist China,
     1945–1963: A Medicine of Revolution* (London and New
     York, 2005), p. 16.

95   Ibid., p. 120.

96   Unschuld, *Medicine in China: A History of Ideas*, pp. 252–
     60.

97   The name 'Great Leap Forward' was the term for the second
     Five Year Plan of the People's Republic. It was intended to
     apply from 1958 to 1963 and to align the various levels of
     economic and social development and ideological aware-
     ness in the cities and rural areas, between 'brain workers'
     and 'manual workers', as well as between industry and agri-
     culture. It was also supposed to make good the backlog to
     the developed industrial nations. The campaign was broken
     off because of its obvious failure in 1961.

98   China specialists have controversially discussed Dikötter's
     extrapolation of Chinese archival documentation of the
     disastrous results of the Great Leap Forward, which led the
     Dutch sinologist to conclude: 'Between 1958 and 1962,
     forty-five million Chinese people were worked, starved
     or beaten to death. Mao Zedong threw his country into a
     frenzy with the Great Leap Forward, an attempt to catch   -
     up with and overtake the Western world in less than fifteen
     years. It led to one of the greatest catastrophes the world has
     ever known.' 'Coercion, terror and systematic violence were
     the foundation of the Great Leap Forward. Thanks to the
     often meticulous reports compiled by the party itself, we

can infer that between 1958 and 1962 by a rough approxi-mation 6 to 8 per cent of the victims were tortured to death or summarily killed – amounting to a least 2.5 million peo-ple. Other victims were deliberately deprived of food and starved to death. Many more vanished because they spoke out or simply because they were not liked, for whatever reason, by the man who wielded the ladle in the canteen. Countless people were killed indirectly through neglect, as local cadres were under pressure to focus on figures rather than on people, making sure they fulfilled the targets they were handed by the top planners.' Frank Dikötter, *Mao's Great Famine* (London, New York, Berlin and Sydney, 2011), pp. xii–xiii and back cover.

99 See also Susan Greenhalgh, *Just One Child: Science and Policy in Deng's China* (Berkeley and Los Angeles, CA, 2008).

100 In August 2012 Pan-Wei Pan received the QMCM Quantum Communication Award 2012 'for his Pioneering Achieve-ments in the Realization of Quantum Communication and Multiphoton Entanglement'. http://qcmc2012.org, accessed 19 November 2012.

101 Jerry Guo and Hao Xin, 'Chinese Gene Therapy. Splicing Out the West? *Science*, CCCXIV/5803 (24 November 2006), pp. 1232–5.

102 Hu Shi, *The Development of the Logical Method in Ancient China* [1917] (Shanghai, 1922), online at http://archive.org, accessed 19 November 2012.

103 Ibid.

104 Iwo Amelung, 'Naming Physics: The Strife to Delineate a Field of Modern Science in Late Imperial China', in *Mapping Meanings: Translating Western Knowledge into Late Imperial China*, ed. Michael Lackner and Natascha Vittinghoff (Leiden, 2004), pp. 381–422.

105 Iwo Amelung, 'Die "Vier Grossen Erfindungen": Selbstzweifel und Selbstbestätigung in der chinesischen Wissenschafts- und Technikgeschichtsschreibung', in *Selbstbehauptungsdiskurse in Asien: China – Japan – Korea*, ed. Iwo Amelung, Matthias Koch, Joachim Kurtz, Eun-Jeung Lee and Sven Saaler (Munich, 2003), pp. 243–74.

106 Quoted in Amelung, 'Shaping the Picture of 'Chinese Optics'.

107 I am grateful to Iwo Amelung for this information.

108 Personal recollection of Dr Wilhelm Mann.
109 Quoted in Jiri Hudecek, 'Construction of Traditional Chinese Mathematics in the 20th Century, Wu Wen-Tsun and the Rest', lecture given on 28 July 2011 at the 13th International Conference on the History of Science in East Asia, in Hefei/Anhui, P.R. of China.
110 See the German translation of the original English lecture in Stiftung Mercator, ed., *Aufklärung im Dialog. Eine deutsch-chinesische Annäherung* (Essen, 2013), p. 35.
111 Jiang Xueqin, 'The Test Chinese Schools Still Fail: High Scores for Shanghai's 15-year-olds are Actually a Sign of Weakness', *Wall Street Journal*, Europe Edition, 8 December 2010, at http://online.wsj.com, accessed 8 March 2013.
112 For further information on German missionary activity in China, see also the motives of the Protestant theologian, colonial functionary and political commentator Paul Rohrbach (1869–1956): 'Rohrbach combined colonial and missionary goals and tasks. He supported a new, theologically founded German global power policy and was considered a proponent of a liberal imperialism. His catchy phrases as a theologian fit the purposes of politicians and colonial officials well: Regarding an external cultural policy – that could rake in enormously profitable results – as a religious assignment and duty was something that could gain very broad support.' Hartmut Walravens, 'Letters from Paul Rohrbach to Richard and Salome Wilhelm', *Monumenta Serica. Journal of Oriental Studies*, LVIII (2010), p. 296.

Index